THE BRUMBACK LIBRARY
OF VAN WERT COUNTY
VAN WERT, OHIO

The Roaring Twenties

Titles in the World History Series

The Age of Augustus
The Age of Feudalism
The Age of Pericles
The Alamo
America in the 1960s
The American Frontier
The American Revolution
Ancient Greece
The Ancient Near East
Architecture
Aztec Civilization
The Battle of the
    Little Bighorn
The Black Death
The Byzantine Empire
Caesar's Conquest of Gaul
The California Gold Rush
The Chinese Cultural
    Revolution
The Civil Rights Movement
The Collapse of the
    Roman Republic
The Conquest of Mexico
The Crimean War
The Crusades
The Cuban Missile Crisis
The Cuban Revolution
The Early Middle Ages
Egypt of the Pharaohs
Elizabethan England
The End of the Cold War
The French and Indian War
The French Revolution
The Glorious Revolution
The Great Depression
Greek and Roman
    Mythology
Greek and Roman Science

Greek and Roman Theater
The History of Slavery
Hitler's Reich
The Hundred Years' War
The Industrial Revolution
The Inquisition
The Italian Renaissance
The Late Middle Ages
The Lewis and Clark
    Expedition
The Mexican Revolution
The Mexican War of
    Independence
Modern Japan
The Mongol Empire
The Persian Empire
The Punic Wars
The Reformation
The Relocation of the
    North American Indian
The Renaissance
The Roaring Twenties
The Roman Empire
The Roman Republic
Roosevelt and the New Deal
The Russian Revolution
Russia of the Tsars
The Scientific Revolution
The Spread of Islam
The Stone Age
Traditional Africa
Traditional Japan
The Travels of Marco Polo
Twentieth Century Science
The Wars of the Roses
The Watts Riot
Women's Suffrage

WORLD HISTORY SERIES ■ ■ ■

The Roaring Twenties

by
David Pietrusza

973.91
PIE

Lucent Books, P.O. Box 289011, San Diego, CA 92198-9011

JH VWM VWM

Library of Congress Cataloging-in-Publication Data

Pietrusza, David, 1949–
    The roaring twenties / by David Pietrusza.
       p. cm.—(World history series)
    Includes bibliographical references (p.   ) and index.
    Summary: Presents a social history of the United States
during the 1920s, a decade of prosperity, Prohibition,
presidential scandals, fads and sensations, controversies,
sports heroes, and the stock market crash.
    ISBN 1-56006-309-2 (alk. paper)
    1. United States—History—1919–1933—Juvenile literature.
[1. United States—History—1919–1933.] I. Title. II. Series.
E784.P5   1998
973.91—dc21   97-29771
                                     CIP
                                      AC

17.96

Contents

Foreword

Each year on the first day of school, nearly every history teacher faces the task of explaining why his or her students should study history. One logical answer to this question is that exploring what happened in our past explains how the things we often take for granted—our customs, ideas, and institutions—came to be. As statesman and historian Winston Churchill put it, "Every nation or group of nations has its own tale to tell. Knowledge of the trials and struggles is necessary to all who would comprehend the problems, perils, challenges, and opportunities which confront us today." Thus, a study of history puts modern ideas and institutions in perspective. For example, though the founders of the United States were talented and creative thinkers, they clearly did not invent the concept of democracy. Instead, they adapted some democratic ideas that had originated in ancient Greece and with which the Romans, the British, and others had experimented. An exploration of these cultures, then, reveals their very real connection to us through institutions that continue to shape our daily lives.

Another reason often given for studying history is the idea that lessons exist in the past from which contemporary societies can benefit and learn. This idea, although controversial, has always been an intriguing one for historians. Those who agree that society can benefit from the past often quote philosopher George Santayana's famous statement, "Those who cannot remember the past are condemned to repeat it." Historians who ascribe to Santayana's philosophy believe that, for example, studying the events that led up to the major world wars or other significant historical events would allow society to chart a different and more favorable course in the future.

Just as difficult as convincing students to realize the importance of studying history is the search for useful and interesting supplementary materials that present historical events in a context that can be easily understood. The volumes in Lucent Books' World History Series attempt to present a broad, balanced, and penetrating view of the march of history. Ancient Egypt's important wars and rulers, for example, are presented against the rich and colorful backdrop of Egyptian religious, social, and cultural developments. The series engages the reader by enhancing historical events with these cultural contexts. For example, in *Ancient Greece*, the text covers the role of women in that society. Slavery is discussed in *The Roman Empire*, as well as how slaves earned their freedom. The numerous and varied aspects of everyday life in these and other societies are explored in each volume of the series. Additionally, the series covers the major political, cultural, and philosophical ideas as the torch of civilization is passed from ancient Mesopotamia and Egypt, through Greece, Rome, Medieval Europe, and other world cultures, to the modern day.

The material in the series is formatted in a thorough, precise, and organized manner. Each volume offers the reader a comprehensive and clearly written overview of an important historical event or period. The topic under discussion is placed in a broad historical context. For example, *The Italian Renaissance* begins with a discussion of the High Middle Ages and the loss of central control that allowed certain Italian cities to develop artistically. The book ends by looking forward to the Reformation and interpreting the societal changes that grew out of the Renaissance. Thus, students are not only involved in an historical era, but also enveloped by the events leading up to that era and the events following it.

One important and unique feature in the World History Series is the primary and secondary source quotations that richly supplement each volume. These quotes are useful in a number of ways. First, they allow students access to sources they would not normally be exposed to because of the difficulty and obscurity of the original source. The quotations range from interesting anecdotes to farsighted cultural perspectives and are drawn from historical witnesses both past and present. Second, the quotes demonstrate how and where historians themselves derive their information on the past as they strive to reach a consensus on historical events. Lastly, all of the quotes are footnoted, familiarizing students with the citation process and allowing them to verify quotes and/or look up the original source if the quote piques their interest.

Finally, the books in the World History Series provide a detailed launching point for further research. Each book contains a bibliography specifically geared toward student research. A second, annotated bibliography introduces students to all the sources the author consulted when compiling the book. A chronology of important dates gives students an overview, at a glance, of the topic covered. Where applicable, a glossary of terms is included.

In short, the series is designed not only to acquaint readers with the basics of history, but also to make them aware that their lives are a part of an ongoing human saga. Perhaps they will then come to the same realization as famed historian Arnold Toynbee. In his monumental work, *A Study of History*, he wrote about becoming aware of history flowing through him in a mighty current, and of his own life "welling like a wave in the flow of this vast tide."

Important Dates in the History of the Roaring Twenties

1919	1920	1921	1922	1923	1924

1919
Eighteenth Amendment to the Constitution bans the manufacture, sale, and transport of intoxicating liquors in the United States; Jack Dempsey wins heavyweight boxing title; members of the Chicago White Sox are paid by gamblers to lose the World Series; U.S. Congress rejects invitation to join the League of Nations (November 19).

1919–1920
U.S. Attorney General Palmer carries out "Red Scare."

1920
Red Sox announce sale of Babe Ruth to Yankees; Prohibition goes into effect; Al Capone murders Big Jim Colosimo; Big Bill Tilden wins first Wimbledon title; Sin-clair Lewis publishes *Main Street;* National Football League (NFL) founded; first successful commercial radio station (KDKA in Pittsburgh) goes on the air; Warren G. Harding elected president, to succeed Woodrow Wilson.

1921
President Harding establishes Bureau of the Budget (June 10); Dempsey fights Georges Carpentier (July 2); Nicola Sacco and Bartolomeo Vanzetti, penniless Italian immigrants, are convicted of a holdup murder in proceedings many see as unjust; players accused in World Series scandal are banned from baseball; first baseball broadcast takes place; Rudolph Valentino stars in *Four Horsemen of the Apocalypse* and *The Sheik;* Charlie Chaplin stars in *The Kid.*

1922
Abie's Irish Rose opens on Broadway; Sinclair Lewis publishes *Babbitt;* Louis Armstrong joins King Oliver's Creole Jazz Band.

1923
Yankee Stadium opens; President Harding dies, is succeeded by Calvin Coolidge; Helen Wills wins first of seven U.S. women's tennis titles; Dempsey defeats Luis Firpo.

1924
Paul Whiteman conducts first performance of George Gershwin's *Rhapsody in Blue;* Ku Klux Klan peaks at 3 million members; Congress investigates the Teapot Dome scandal; Nathan Leopold and Richard Loeb mur-

| 1925 | 1926 | 1927 | 1928 | 1929 | 1930 |

der Bobby Franks; Secretary of the Interior Albert B. Fall indicted; Congress restricts immigration; Attorney General Harry Daugherty resigns under fire; Calvin Coolidge elected president.

1925
Charlie Chaplin makes *The Gold Rush;* John T. Scopes is tried for teaching evolution; William Jennings Bryan dies; Ku Klux Klan marches in Washington; F. Scott Fitzgerald publishes *The Great Gatsby;* H. L. Mencken and George Jean Nathan found *The American Mercury;* Red Grange joins the National Football League; Chicago mobster Dion O'Banion is murdered.

1926
Suzanne Lenglen defeats Helen Wills at Cannes;

National Broadcasting Company (NBC) is formed; Gertrude Ederle swims the English Channel; Valentino dies; Dempsey loses heavyweight crown to Gene Tunney.

1927
Charles A. Lindberg flies from New York to Paris; Sacco and Vanzetti executed; Tunney again defeats Dempsey; Babe Ruth hits his sixtieth home run; *The Jazz Singer* premieres; Sinclair Lewis publishes *Elmer Gantry;* Federal Radio Commission regulates radio frequencies; Columbia Broadcasting System (CBS) is formed; the Cotton Club opens in Harlem.

1928
Herbert Hoover defeats Al Smith for the presi-

dency; Franklin Roosevelt is elected governor of New York.

1929
Five of Al Capone's rivals are killed in the St. Valentine's Day Massacre (February 14); Albert B. Fall convicted (October 25); stock market crashes (October 29).

1930
Unemployment reaches 4 to 5 million; Hoover signs Hawley-Smoot Act, a strict protectionist tariff.

The Decade That Roared

The decade of the 1920s is widely known as "the Roaring Twenties" for good reason. It romped, rampaged, and rioted like no other decade before or since.

The times were peaceful (World War I had just ended in 1918), and in America, business boomed. The country had known prosperity before—but now Americans had an outlook on life far different from that of their parents and grandparents. People were no longer satisfied to work hard and save money. In this prosperous era, more and more Americans used newfound wealth to move away from many traditional inhibitions and restrictions. American industry produced more conveniences, and the people wanted to own them.

Good Times

But Americans desired more than a standard of living based on a modest home and an assortment of appliances. They wanted a good time—and they had one. Radios, talking pictures, and owning an automobile were within the grasp of the middle class, even if they had to buy on credit—a concept also invented in the twenties. Average people invested in the stock market and sidestepped a nationwide ban on intoxicating liquors by making gin in their bathtubs and buying beer from illegal distributors called bootleggers. Huge new stadiums and grandly ornate motion picture palaces were built, and athletes and movie stars became heroes. It was an era when Americans had *fun*—a holiday they thought would never end.

America's growing industry boosted '20s prosperity by providing jobs on a mass scale. "The greater the profit, the greater the wages,"[1] future president Calvin Coolidge had declared at the dawn of the decade. Business leaders were well known and admired, particularly auto magnate Henry Ford and engineer-statesman Herbert Hoover.

In the United States, the central event of the '20s was Prohibition. In 1919 the U.S. Constitution had been amended to ban booze, but a huge segment of society seemed determined to spend the next decade looking for illicit alcohol. Before the ratification of the Eighteenth Amendment, many people in the middle class tended to frown on drinking. But once Prohibition arrived, drinking became fashionable. More members of the middle class, more college students—and more women—drank in clublike establishments called speakeasies. Bootleggers went into business to provide drinkers with beer and

Epitomizing the wealth and glamour of the Roaring Twenties, a young woman poses for a photograph beside her sporty roadster.

liquor. Profits were big and attracted the worst elements in society. Prohibition fueled the growth of organized crime, as big city gangsters battled for turf, often riddling their rivals with machine-gun bullets. Police officers were bribed to overlook gang violence, speakeasies, and the activities of bootleggers. Respect for law enforcement dwindled.

Gangsters and corrupt police officers were not the only ones breaking the law. A number of major breaches of public trust rocked society. The Teapot Dome scandal, a complex web of bribery and misuse of power by government officials, resulted in three cabinet members leaving office in disgrace. Members of the Chicago White Sox rigged a World Series.

If dishonesty on the part of public figures was being revealed with alarming frequency, an equally disturbing trend was the growth of anti-immigrant sentiment among average Americans.

Millions of Europeans and Asians had come to the United States in the decades before 1920. Now Americans were increasingly

Police officers in Washington chase a bootlegger's car, which is equipped with a smoke-screen device.

suspicious of foreigners—and moved to severely limit immigration from eastern and southern Europe and Japan. In Massachusetts, two Italian-born anarchists, Nicola Sacco and Bartolomeo Vanzetti, were charged with armed robbery and murder. Many political progressives saw them as victims of prejudice and battled unsuccessfully for their freedom.

The 1920s ended not with a roar but with a bang. On "Black Tuesday," October 29, 1929, the stock market crashed and took the world's economy with it. The Great Depression that followed the collapse of the securities market would last throughout the 1930s, making the fun-loving decade that had gone before seem like a dream. Boom times disappeared, replaced by desperate poverty. Americans looked toward the federal government—and not to business leaders—for assistance and stability.

1 Boom Times: The Economy Roars

Although the Roaring Twenties were times of unprecedented prosperity, the decade began with a severe postwar depression. The war was World War I, and when it was over, American industry no longer needed to produce armaments. At the same time that the armistice, or cease-fire, was eliminating thousands of jobs, millions of returning soldiers flooded the job market. High wartime taxes and cumbersome wartime regulations further slowed recovery. Unemployment and inflation grew. In 1920 Americans rejected the party of outgoing two-term Democratic president Woodrow Wilson and elected an Ohio Republican, Warren Gamaliel Harding, in hopes that he could turn the economy around.

Tax and Budget Cutting

Harding took office in March 1921. In January 1921, 3,473,446 were unemployed. Some experts estimated that translated into a jobless rate of 20 percent. By the end of 1921, 4,754,000 were unemployed.

President Warren G. Harding steps off a train. Harding was elected at the start of the 1920s in hopes that he could revive America's failing economy.

Yet by the spring of 1922 the nation started to pull out of hard times. The government began an aggressive program to reduce inflation, eliminate wartime regulations, and lower taxes and government expenditures. Harding not only saw to it that there were cuts in federal spending to correspond to the phasing out of programs needed for World War I, he lowered spending below what it had been before the war. Harding had been able to accomplish this by reforming the federal budget process and creating a Bureau of the Budget, the forerunner of the OMB (Office of Management and Budget).

By July 1922 an economic recovery had begun. Prosperity steadily grew to historic highs. In August 1923 President Harding died of a heart attack, but his successor, Calvin "Silent Cal" Coolidge continued his policies and the boom times continued.

Coolidge had one central idea concerning government—economy in spending and the removal of the high income tax rates enacted during the war. He believed that these high rates were counterproductive and were shifting the tax burden from the rich to the poor. "If the rates of large incomes are so high that [large incomes] disappear," he once remarked, "the small taxpayer will be left to bear the entire burden. If on the other hand, the rates are placed where they will secure the most revenue from large incomes, then the small taxpayer will be relieved."[2]

By 1929 the tax rate on the first $7,500 in income (a very good income for the time) had been reduced to just 1.5 percent, with an exemption on the first $1,500 in income for single persons and $3,500 for a married couple or a head of household. The very most a married couple

A campaign poster supports the election of Calvin Coolidge and his running mate, Charles G. Dawes. Coolidge believed that income tax had to be reduced to allow the economy to boom.

might pay in federal income tax was $60 a year. At $12,000 the rate jumped to 5 percent. For the very rich there was a surcharge that gradually grew to 20 percent on incomes over $100,000. "It is only a tiny exaggeration," notes historian Thomas B. Silver in *Coolidge and the Historians*, "to say that Coolidge and [Treasury secretary Andrew W.] Mellon completely removed the burden of federal income taxation from the backs of poor and working people between the time Coolidge entered the presidency and the time he left."[3]

The gross national product increased from $59.4 billion in 1921 to $87.2 billion in 1929—factory production nearly doubled. In the same time period per capita American income grew from $522 to $716. "Under Harding and still more under Coolidge," historian Paul Johnson reports in *Modern Times*, "the USA enjoyed a general prosperity which was historically unique in its experience or that of any other society."[4]

Business Trends

Chain stores (as opposed to locally owned, "mom-and-pop" businesses) had existed for several decades. But in the 1920s they grew greatly in popularity, as rising incomes brought about an increase in consumer activity. The A&P grocery store chain, for example, increased from 4,621 stores in 1920 to 15,418 in 1928; Piggly Wiggly outlets went from 515 to 2,500; J. C. Penney grew from 312 to 1,395, and S. S. Kresge (now Kmart) from 184 to 597. Much of the attraction was due to the cheaper prices offered by the chains. In 1921 a Piggly Wiggly customer could purchase three pounds of a name brand coffee for just $1.05; a typical locally owned store, whose owners had neither the funds nor the storage space to be able to buy in bulk, like the chains, had to charge $1.55 for the same item.

Chain stores (as well as other businesses in the 1920s) also relied on other sales techniques to attract customers. One of the most important changes was the increased use of buying on credit, by making it easy to obtain, payments small, and interest low. Previously, most consumers had been very hesitant to borrow money for purchases. They were greatly ashamed to be in debt. With a renewed faith in a prosperous economy, many Americans rushed into stores to put 10 percent down and pay the rest in monthly installments. By 1929 Americans were spending $7 billion a year in installment outlays. In 1929 half of all appliance purchases and two-thirds of auto purchases were made on credit or installment buying.

Buying on installment allowed one industry to experience remarkable growth during the 1920s: by 1929, five out of every six cars made in the world were made in America, and approximately one in five Americans owned a car. And automobile ownership carried with it a feeling of personal freedom that was important to the fun-loving people of the Roaring Twenties.

". . . As Long as It Is Black"

About half the U.S.-made autos were Fords. No one had been more responsible for bringing the automobile into the price range of the average American than Detroit's Henry Ford. A former mechanic,

Crowds take advantage of a glove sale in a department store in 1926. In the 1920s, small independently owned department stores gave way to chain stores.

Ford had founded the Ford Motor Company in 1903 and, by pioneering the assembly line, he drastically reduced the cost of his Model T (or "Tin Lizzy," as many called the cheaply made car). Thus the Ford automobile—and later other makers' automobiles—could be sold at prices average Americans felt they could afford. Eventually Ford manufactured and sold 15 million Model Ts.

Although many now-vanished automakers existed in the 1920s, one company that not only survived the decade but became Ford's main competitor was General Motors. GM offered consumers a greater variety of models (including Buick, Cadillac, Oldsmobile, Chevrolet, and LaSalle), more features, and even colors. Another growing auto company was Chrysler Motors (founded by Walter P. Chrysler, a former GM executive). *Time* magazine recognized Walter Chrysler's rapid rise and named him its Man of the Year for 1928. By 1929

Chrysler Motors was manufacturing 700,000 cars a year (compared to GM's 1 million), including the Chrysler, the Dodge, the Plymouth, and the DeSoto.

Despite such competition, Henry Ford stubbornly resisted changing his once innovative methods—not even wanting to make the famous Model T available in colors. "The customer," he responded, "can have a Ford any color he wants—as long as it is black."[5] But Ford had to bow to changing times, and in December 1927 he finally abandoned his beloved Model T in favor of an updated version, the Model A. Four hundred thousand orders poured in immediately.

A Risky Market

Besides purchasing more items on credit, Americans participated on a massive scale

"Economy Is Idealism in Its Most Practical Form"

In the 1920s many credited President Calvin Coolidge's strict frugality in government spending and reluctance to add to the people's tax burden with helping to create conditions that made boom times possible. At his inauguration in March 1925, the Vermont-born Coolidge outlined his thoughts on the subject. The quote is taken from the CD Sourcebook of American History.

"The policy that stands out with the greatest clearness is that of economy in public expenditure with reduction and reform of taxation. The principle involved in this effort is that of conservation. The resources of this country are almost beyond computation. No mind can comprehend them. But the cost of our combined governments is likewise almost beyond definition. Not only those who are now making their tax returns, but those who meet the enhanced cost of existence in their monthly bills, know by hard experience what this great burden is and what it does. No matter what others may want, these people want a drastic economy [cutting back of expenses]. They are opposed to waste. They know that extravagance lengthens the hours and diminishes the rewards of their labor. I favor the policy of economy, not because I wish to save money, but because I wish to save people. The men and women of this country who toil are the ones who bear the cost of the Government. Every dollar that we carelessly waste means that their life will be so much the more meager. Every dollar that we prudently save means that their life will be so much the more abundant. Economy is idealism in its most practical form. . . .

The wisest and soundest method of solving our tax problem is through economy. Fortunately, of all the great nations this country is best in a position to adopt that simple remedy. We do not any longer need war-time revenues. The collection of any taxes which are not absolutely required, which do not beyond reasonable doubt contribute to the public welfare, is only a species of legalized larceny. Under this republic the rewards of industry belong to those who earn them. The only constitutional tax is the tax which ministers to public necessity. The property of the country belongs to the people of the country. Their title is absolute. They do not support any privileged class; they do not need to maintain great military forces; they ought not to be burdened with a great array of public employees."

in another '20s phenomenon: the stock market. The profits that companies made (and the wages workers and management earned) helped fuel heavy investment—and in many cases, speculation—in stocks.

Many investors made quick profits, but because the market was largely unregulated, it was subject to manipulation by shady brokers. In addition, high levels of speculation by almost everyone—honest and not so honest, experienced and naive—had a distorting effect that made it difficult even for professional analysts to get a clear overall picture.

One factor that increased stock speculation—and greatly magnified the risks involved in investing—was the practice of buying shares of stock "on margin," a form of credit purchase. Often 10 percent down was sufficient to open an investment ac-

Brokers examine the boards of the New York Stock Exchange. Americans participated in the stock market on a massive scale during the 1920s.

Henry Ford pioneered the assembly line during the 1920s, making his cars far more affordable to the average American.

count. Brokers, eager to sell more and more stock so they could maximize their commissions, borrowed money from banks to be able to lend their clients the rest of the money needed for margin purchases. Normally, when a person took out a loan, some collateral was necessary as security. But when 1920s investors purchased stock "on margin," the stock itself served as collateral. This made the whole operation even more risky.

Suppose a person purchased $100,000 in stock for a margin of $10,000. This buyer would actually own only the margin amount of $10,000. If share prices went up, on paper, at least, the investor was ahead of the game, and the bank would not be in a hurry to call in the loan. But if the market stagnated—or worse yet, went *down*—disaster was possible. Margin loans were payable at any time, at the demand of

"The Genius of Modern America"

When auto manu-facturer Henry Ford introduced his new Model A in December 1927, the event caught everyone's attention and reminded people how Ford had revolution-ized the industry. This editorial from the New York World *is reprinted in James Boylan's* The World and the 20s.

"What would be guesswork on the part of other men is exact calculation to Mr. Ford; he has succeeded in making the automobile business as scientific as the engineer has succeeded in making the business of driving a tunnel. . . . Indeed, [Mr. Ford] appears as the genius of modern America. The thing which he makes is surely the symbol of the advance which the modern age has made over any other age. And the way he makes it, with efficiency calculated to the nth degree, with a vast organization by means of which, as he says, 'we make our own steel—we make our own glass—we mine our own coal—we make virtually every part used in the Ford car'—that is what we like to think marks off America as superior in at least one respect to the rest of the world. Other people may make better music than we make, better rugs, better singers, better ships. But at the business of making a great machine of steel and men and making it work we acknowledge no superior, and we believe that is our contribution to civilization. And Mr. Ford personifies it better than any man living."

Ford's Model T. The industrialist's pioneering methods allowed many more Americans to afford automobiles.

the lender. Thus if the value of our buyer's stock dropped 25 percent, to $75,000, trouble was in sight. A broker, unable to pay back his loans to the bank, would demand that the investor come up with $90,000—plus interest—to pay off the rest of the amount due on the purchase of stock. Often that money simply was not there—and buyers who could not pay were ruined financially. When a great many investors went bust at the same time, the market itself was subject to collapse.

Another risk to investors who bought on margin was the high interest brokers and bankers charged for the loans that made up the purchase price. In the 1920s interest rates were normally 4 percent, but investors who borrowed to buy stocks on margin usually paid 12 percent. Paying back the interest, on top of the principal, or loan amount, was virtually impossible for the average investor surprised by a drop in stock prices.

Wall Street brokers not only used aggressive tactics to sell stock on margin, a risky but legal practice, but some resorted to such outright unethical maneuvers as joining together in a "pool" to artificially force the price of a particular stock to higher levels. They would invest heavily in the stock at relatively low prices, thus creating an untrue impression of its value. Investors not in on the scheme would then be encouraged to buy the stock at the inflated price. As share prices continued to climb, the "pool" would sell out, making huge profits, and new investors would often lose their life savings when the stock tumbled back to its fair market value.

The dream of easy profits lured many persons to buy stocks on margin. It seemed that *everyone* was making money in the stock market—and for a while a great many people actually were. Thus people who had not yet invested wanted to get in on the action, although in many cases these latecomers had very little understanding of the risks they were taking. Whereas 223 million shares were traded on Wall Street in 1920, by 1927 that figure had soared to 576 million. By 1929 it would reach 1,124,000,000—breaching the billion-share mark for the first time. In the first nine months of 1929, there were 300 million *new* shares traded on Wall

Street. Borrowing to buy stocks rose just as fast. Brokers' loans rose from $3 billion in 1926 to $8.5 billion in September 1929.

More and more people became investors. Some wanted security for their old age. Others were more adventurous: they wanted to get *rich*. And there seemed to be no good reason not to be rich. In August 1929 General Motors executive (and former chairman of the Democratic National Committee) John Jacob Raskob advised Americans in a *Ladies' Home Journal* interview how to get in on the money making. If one were to invest just $15 per month in common stock, he stated, the result in twenty years would be $80,000. That, in turn, would yield $400 in interest per month—enough to live on in those days. "I am firm in my belief that anyone not only can be rich," Raskob concluded, "but ought to be rich."[6]

Hard Times for Some

Not everyone could afford to invest in the stock market. Not everyone could afford a shiny new Model T or Buick. And not everyone shared in the prosperity of the Roaring Twenties. Farmers, New England textile workers, and many southerners—both black and white—were among those who lagged behind economically. Farmers were particularly hard hit. During World War I Europeans had to buy huge amounts of grain and meat from America. This caused farm prices—and profits—to rise dramatically. But after the war, Europeans went back to farm production, and the need for agricultural imports from the United States fell substantially. As a result, American farm income dropped by $3 billion. Farmers

A child picks cotton in the South. While the 1920s was a decade of unprecedented prosperity, farmers, especially black sharecroppers, did not share in the economic boom.

had less money to live on and less money to pay back loans for farm equipment and supplies. New agricultural techniques (such as the use of tractors) had made farming easier but had also increased farm surpluses and depressed the prices farmers could get for their crops. By 1929 U.S. farmers were $10 billion in debt.

In the South many farmers were in dire straits. Particularly distressed were the farmers who did not own land—the "sharecroppers," working other people's land in exchange for a "share" of the crop. Sixty-one percent of black farmers in the South were sharecroppers; in Georgia the figure was 80 percent.

In the 1920s, only 10 percent of farms had electricity and hundreds of thousands of farmers fled the poverty of rural life. They moved either to industrialized northern cities or small southern towns built up around textile mills. The mills paid extremely low wages and worked their employees long hours. Conditions were often unhealthy and dangerous. But, observes historian Joe Alex Morris in *What a Year!*, "Compared to the shanties in which [the former sharecroppers] had grown up, some company villages erected near the mills in Southern towns seemed like luxury to many . . . and the pay represented more cash in a month or so than most had ever seen in a year."[7]

Employees who fixed textile looms in Massachusetts, for example, earned a wage of 62 cents per hour; in North Carolina the same work paid just 42 cents. Taxes were also lower in the South. "Move That Mill Down South," an ad paid for by the state government of Alabama urged, "Then Pay Your Dividends From the Taxes Saved."[8] This combination of lower wages and taxes caused many manufacturers to abandon their New England mills, leaving thousands of Yankee workers without jobs.

"The Poorhouse Is Vanishing from Among Us"

Although the Roaring Twenties were indeed characterized by poverty for some and irresponsible spending by others, a large share of Americans' money went toward the public good. The prosperous national economy was raising living standards, health standards, and educational standards. By 1928 the United States spent as much on education as the rest of the world combined. More American children

The Declining Job Market

Throughout Massachusetts the number of persons working in the state's textile and shoe manufacturing mill towns dropped significantly.

City	Number of Manufacturing Jobs	
	in 1923	in 1926
Haverhill	12,673	11,917
Brockton	15,205	12,762
New Bedford	37,917	35,143
Fall River	37,018	31,353
Lawrence	35,292	26,777
Lowell	27,162	20,859

had a chance at a decent education. In 1900 only 10 percent of all children went to high school; by 1931 that number had increased to 50 percent.

American health improved greatly. In the 1920s the average life span grew from forty-nine years to fifty-nine years. Infant mortality declined by two-thirds. Deadly diseases such as diphtheria and typhoid were controlled as never before.

Although many in the country were poor, it was widely believed that the boom times would spread to them, as well. "We in America today are nearer to the final triumph over poverty than ever before in the history of any land," presidential nominee Herbert Hoover told the Republican National Convention in 1928. "The poorhouse is vanishing from among us. We have not yet reached that goal, but, given a chance to go forward with the policies of the last eight years, we shall soon, with the help of God, be in sight of the day when poverty shall be banished from this nation."[9]

Chapter

2 Prohibition: The Wettest Dry Nation Ever

In the 1920s America began a bold new social experiment—the national prohibition of alcohol. For decades Americans had wrestled with the issue of how to control the problems brought on by alcohol abuse, which included ruined careers, ruined marriages, and untold numbers of ruined lives. Antialcohol crusaders believed that saloons were bad places; men who patronized them not only drank to excess but also lost their weekly earnings at gambling, and met prostitutes, from whom they contracted venereal disease. Criminals gathered in saloons to hatch illegal schemes. In the nineteenth century, antialcohol activists moved from urging temperance (controlled and

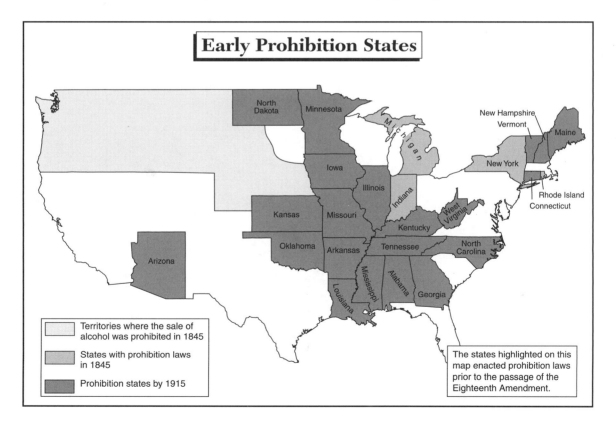

Early Prohibition States

Territories where the sale of alcohol was prohibited in 1845

States with prohibition laws in 1845

Prohibition states by 1915

The states highlighted on this map enacted prohibition laws prior to the passage of the Eighteenth Amendment.

sensible drinking) to advocating prohibition, or the outright ban on the sale of alcohol and the abolition of the saloon.

At first supporters of Prohibition (the movement collectively was referred to with a capital "P") did not work at the federal level; mostly they lobbied state and local governments. By 1890 seven states had passed statewide prohibition of alcoholic beverages and twenty-three others allowed local communities to ban the sale of alcohol. There was no serious movement to enact this policy nationwide, however, until 1913. In December of that year, the Anti-Saloon League, a prominent prohibitionist organization, went on record supporting such a concept.

Wets vs. Drys

In December 1913—when "drys" (those supporting Prohibition) began to advocate a national liquor ban—neither drys nor "wets" (those who opposed Prohibition)

could have predicted the effect that the outbreak of armed conflict in Europe—that is, World War I—would eventually have on the issue at home. When the United States declared war on Germany and Austria in 1917, patriotic forces were unleashed that would lead to the rapid passage of national Prohibition. Many of America's brewers were of German birth or ancestry and not surprisingly sympathized with their country of origin. The drys tied the issues of patriotism and prohibition together and used widespread anti-German feeling to whip up prohibitionist feelings. Drys also argued that the grain used for brewing beer and distilling hard liquor could better serve the war effort by being made into bread and used to manufacture other badly needed foodstuffs. Prohibitionists also pointed out the need for sobriety in the armed forces and in the defense plants.

For all these reasons, congressional support for outlawing alcohol grew quickly. On December 18, 1917, the House of Representatives wanted to make Prohibition

The Women's Christian Temperance Union participates in a march in 1914. Women lobbied for the prohibition of alcohol because many men squandered money on liquor, leaving their wives and children to go hungry.

"The Manufacture, Sale, or Transportation of Intoxicating Liquors"

A lot has been written about Prohibition, but it took up only three paragraphs in the U.S. Constitution. This is what the Eighteenth Amendment said.

"Section 1. After one year from the ratification of this article the manufacture, sale, or transportation of intoxicating liquors within, the importation thereof into, or the exportation thereof from the United States and all territory subject to the jurisdiction thereof for beverage purposes is hereby prohibited.

Section 2. The Congress and the several States shall have concurrent power to enforce this article by appropriate legislation.

Section 3. This article shall be inoperative unless it shall have been ratified as an amendment to the Constitution by the legislatures of the several States, as provided in the Constitution, within seven years from the date of the submission hereof to the States by Congress."

---

the Eighteenth Amendment to the Constitution. Congress sent the amendment to the states for ratification. Two-thirds of the states had to approve the measure within the next seven years for the amendment to take effect. In just thirteen months—in January 1919—enough states had said yes to the Eighteenth Amendment. Another year passed though before the amendment actually took effect. America officially went dry on January 17, 1920.

"This Law Will Be Obeyed . . ."

Prohibitionists had high hopes for a dry future. Perhaps naively, they had expected Americans to quickly turn away from alcohol, whereupon, they trusted, many of the evils that were due to drinking would vanish or at least be dramatically reduced. "This law," said John F. Kramer, commissioner of the Prohibition Bureau (the agency that enforced Prohibition), "will be obeyed in cities large and small, and in villages, and where it is not obeyed, it will be enforced." [10] Others disagreed. They had no confidence at all that America's drinking habits could be changed so easily—particularly in the big cities. New York congressman Fiorello H. LaGuardia, who later became one of New York City's most famous mayors, had this practical comment: "In order to enforce prohibition, it will require a police force of 250,000 men and a force of 250,000 men to police the police." [11]

A car filled with anti-Prohibitionists advertises repealing the Eighteenth Amendment. Once passed, the amendment was nearly impossible to enforce.

LaGuardia's prediction proved far more accurate than Prohibition commissioner Kramer's. Americans evaded the Eighteenth Amendment in almost every conceivable way. For example, it was illegal to manufacture, sell, or transport alcohol, but it was not illegal to *drink* it. A person who merely bought bootleg alcohol could not be arrested for having it in his home and for drinking it. Thus, *consumers* of alcohol generally had little to fear from government authorities. And if they had little to fear, there remained a large market for alcohol. And if a larger number of persons still were willing to *buy* alcohol, a large number of persons were more than willing to *sell* it.

It was also legal to use alcohol for medicinal purposes. Many doctors and pharmacists would hand out prescriptions for "medicinal" alcohol to anyone who asked. Patients or clients of those who refused to comply would simply find someone more flexible, and the law-abiding professionals would lose legitimate business in the bargain.

There was another big loophole, as well. Prohibition was scheduled to take effect on January 29, 1920, one full year after the state that brought the total of ratifiers up to two-thirds had acted. This gave businesses and drinkers, particularly wealthy drinkers, plenty of time to stock up. New York City's prestigious Yale Club stored a fourteen-year supply. "The business of evading Prohibition and making mock of it," wrote journalist H. L. Mencken toward the end of 1926, "has ceased to wear any aspects of crime, and has become a sort of national sport."[12]

Prohibition merely replaced the saloon with the "speakeasy" (so-called because people who drank there spoke "easy" or quietly as they entered). Speakeasies (sometimes known as blind pigs) were establishments in which illegal alcohol was sold and consumed. During Prohibition they were almost everywhere, particularly in the larger cities. New York, for example, claimed five thousand speakeasies by 1922 and over thirty-two thousand by 1926. It seemed just about everybody was going into the business. "All you need is two bottles and a room and you have a speakeasy,"[13] noted the city's police commissioner, Grover A. Whalen.

In many cases the speakeasies were far worse than the old saloon. Because the manufacture of alcohol was illegal, the drinks speakeasies served were likely to contain hazardous substances such as wood alcohol. Although wood alcohol produces an intoxicating effect like that of ethyl alcohol, the principal ingredient of beverages sold legally today, consumption of relatively small amounts of this substitute could lead to blindness or death. In

"He Turned His Drugstore into a Speak-Easy"

Not only gangsters and bootleggers supplied illicit alcohol during Prohibition. Many respectable doctors and druggists did the same. In The Amazing Story of Repeal, *Fletcher Dobyns gives this account.*

"A still more tragic result was the fact that large numbers of normally honest and law-abiding physicians and druggists felt the law was so drawn that its violation was forced upon them. . . . If a man asked for a liquor prescription, it was the duty of the physician to refuse it unless he honestly believed that the man was suffering from 'some known ailment' for which an alcoholic beverage was a proper remedy. He knew, however, that if he took this course, the man would not only resent it but also go to some more accommodating physician for his liquor supply. He feared that he would not only lose the money which he would have received for the liquor prescription, which he was willing to do, but that he would lose the man's legitimate patronage [and then he would reason], 'Well, he will get his liquor anyway, and I am not going to sacrifice my practice to a sentimental and futile obedience to a foolish law,' and he lapsed to the status of a bootlegger. . . .

It was comparatively safe . . . for the druggist to furnish liquor to . . . his [discreet] customers. . . . He also knew that if he refused to do so, that he would lose both his liquor[-consuming] and his legitimate patronage. So he turned his drugstore into a speak-easy.

Eventually, in every part of the country, many physicians and druggists who were naturally among the most intelligent and law-abiding people in their communities, became bootleggers and proprietors of speak-easies. They lost all respect for a law which they felt they were forced to violate and their attitude and conduct spread to every class."

addition, in the interest of staying in business, speakeasy owners resorted to widespread bribery of Prohibition agents and local police. Because of the ease with which many Americans flouted the Prohibition act, respect for law and order dropped dramatically during the '20s.

Aiding Americans to obtain illegal booze were hoodlums who branched out from the gambling, prostitution, and extortion rackets and into the bootleg liquor trade because it was so lucrative. "In its practical effects," wrote historian Andrew Sinclair in *Era of Excess*, "national prohibition transferred two billion dollars a year from the hands of brewers, distillers, and shareholders to the hands of murderers, crooks, and illiterates."[14]

Home Brew

It was not difficult for "crooks and illiterates" to go into the booze business. It was really hardly difficult for anyone. Many otherwise law-abiding persons also turned to manufacturing their own alcoholic beverages. There were any number of ways to do so. It was still legal to manufacture and sell nonalcoholic beer (beer with an alcoholic content of less than one-half of 1 percent), and by mixing malt tonic with this form of beer, a beverage with 4 percent alcoholic content could be concocted.

Stills, devices for distilling alcohol from fruit or vegetable materials, could be purchased for as little as $500—a lot of money in the 1920s but a tempting bargain nevertheless when one could make a gallon of booze for fifty cents and sell it for three or four dollars. Just about anything could be used to make alcohol, and the process was quite speedy. "You can take ordinary prunes, raisins, or grapes," said one expert. "You do not have to have hops or malt. You can take ordinary chicken corn, ordinary wheat, ordinary barley, and simplify that with a certain process of cooking and fermentation, and

Two plainclothes policemen raid a speakeasy in 1926. Speakeasies were difficult to shut down, partly because of their sheer numbers.

Three government officials pose with confiscated stills during the 1920s. Alcoholic beverages made with the crude stills may not have been very appealing, but they always packed a "kick."

within 24 hours you can have a fair concoction that will give you a kick. That is all there is in alcohol, a kick."[15]

Wine could also be easily manufactured. Cakes of dried grapes, that could easily be used to make wine, were commonly sold and used to make wine even though they came with a warning how *not* to use them to make wine. Salesmen also issued similar cautions:

> "Yes," they would tell customers, "you simply dissolve this flavored brick in a gallon of warm water, chill and voilà a delicious grape beverage! But be sure not to store this liquid in a cool, dry place for exactly twenty-one days, for then it would turn into wine! And *whatever* you do, *don't* apply this handy cork containing the rubber siphon hose to the neck of the bottle—that procedure would only be used to induce fermentation! Also, be careful not to shake the liquid faithfully once a day, because that, too, will help turn the juice!"[16]

This warning though sounded suspiciously like instructions for violating the Eighteenth Amendment.

Corruption Spreads

Besides providing opportunities for gangsters and amateur bootleggers, Prohibition also gave corrupt police officers and federal officials a chance to get rich. Bootleggers, who dealt in illegal liquor, and rumrunners, who brought alcohol into the country by boat, bought off police officers to ensure that they could conduct business. In Chicago, whose citizens rarely complied with Prohibition, one booze factory operated just four blocks from the Maxwell Street police station. According to the former manager of the operation:

> The warehouse was run openly and in full view of everybody, unmolested by State authorities other than the occasional raid. . . . But notification of 24 hours was always given. . . . Sometimes the very letters sent out by the police ordering the raid were shown [to the bootleggers]. There would be a clean-up, then a raid, then a re-opening. During all the period that I worked there the entire . . . enterprise was done with the full knowledge and approval of the Chicago police.[17]

"You Cannot Carry a Hip Flask"

Contrary to popular belief, Prohibition did not outlaw the possession—or even the consumption—of alcohol. In Prohibition: Thirteen Years That Changed America, *Edward Behr reports how the* New York Daily News *instructed its readers when Prohibition first began.*

"You may drink intoxicating liquor in your own home or in the home of a friend when you are a bona fide guest [really a guest, instead of, say, a customer pretending to be a guest].

You may buy intoxicating liquor on a bona fide medical prescription of a doctor. A pint can be bought every ten days.

You may consider any place you live permanently as your home. If you have more than one home, you may keep a stock of liquor in each.

You may keep liquor in any storage room or club locker, provided the storage place is for the exclusive use of yourself, family or bona fide friends.

You may get a permit to move liquor when you change your residence.

You may manufacture, sell or transport liquor for non-beverage or sacramental [religious] purposes provided you obtain a Government permit.

You cannot carry a hip flask.

You cannot give away or receive a bottle of liquor as a gift.

You cannot take liquor to hotels or restaurants and drink it in the public dining rooms.

You cannot buy or sell formulas or recipes for homemade liquor.

You cannot ship liquor for beverage use.

You cannot manufacture anything above one half of one percent (liquor strength) in your home.

You cannot store liquor in any place except in your own home.

You cannot display liquor signs or advertisements on your premises.

You cannot remove reserve stocks from storage."

The federal government did little to enforce the Eighteenth Amendment. The Prohibition Bureau received inadequate funding. There were far too few federal Prohibition agents to patrol the Mexican and Canadian borders, shut down every bootleg still, or close every speakeasy. The total number of Prohibition agents never reached more than 2,300, and at times was as low as 1,500. The few agents hired, moreover, were ill paid. Salaries ranged between $1,200 and $2,000 per year in 1920 and by 1930 had reached just $2,300. Such low pay tempted many agents to accept graft from bootleggers. One in every twelve Prohibition agents was eventually fired after either being caught accepting graft or being accused of accepting bribes. Many Prohibition agents were also unqualified. They did not have to pass civil service tests to get their jobs and many would not have been able to, owing to poor educational background. Instead they were appointed because of their friendships with politicians. "At present we haven't the right kind of investigators," Assistant Attorney General Mabel Walker Willebrandt contended in 1925. "Many of them are well-meaning sentimentalists and dry, but they can't catch crooks. The sole object of the others has been to appropriate all the graft in sight, and they *won't* catch crooks." [18]

All in all, neither federal nor local authorities would commit the resources necessary to enforce the Volstead Act, the controversial federal law that made the Eighteenth Amendment operational. The state of Maryland refused to pass any enforcement statute. New York, Montana, Wisconsin, and Nevada eventually repealed their laws enforcing Prohibition. Other states kept their "dry" laws on the books but did little to enforce them. In 1927, for example, Utah spent only $160 to catch people who ran afoul of the Eighteenth Amendment. "There was never any serious effort to enforce national prohibition until the early thirties," summed up historian Andrew Sinclair in *Era of Excess*, "and by that time it was too late." [19]

Death Among the Flowers

There was plenty of bootlegging business to go around during Prohibition, but the gangsters who trafficked in illegal booze were greedy and battled each other to monopolize the liquor trade in various parts of American cities and states. The city that witnessed the worst mob violence was Chicago, a town that even before Prohibition had been very profitable for gangsters. Before 1920 Chicago's racketeers made their money from gambling and prostitution, but Prohibition provided huge new opportunities for illegal cash.

The ultimate king of 1920s Chicago gangland was Brooklyn-born Al Capone. Capone started out as a strong-arm thug in New York but in 1919 moved to Chicago to work for fellow mobster Johnny Torrio, who, in turn, took orders from his uncle, South Side mob leader Big Jim Colosimo. Torrio had ambitious plans for himself and Capone. Colosimo, however, did not want anything to do with bootlegging; he was making enough money from his existing rackets. This infuriated the greedy Torrio, who in 1920 ordered Capone to murder his uncle. Capone did just that. Torrio became the new boss of the South Side. Capone became his right-hand man.

The North Side of Chicago belonged to Dion O'Banion, a mobster of Irish descent who had long battled with Torrio and Capone over control of the city's bootlegging operations. Finally, in May 1924, O'Banion told Torrio and Capone he was getting out of the bootlegging business. He offered to sell his South Side rivals the huge Sieben brewery in the city's North Side for $500,000. Torrio and Capone jumped at the chance but were quickly double-crossed. As soon as O'Banion had their money, he prevailed on friends on the police force to raid the place and destroy its equipment. Then O'Banion insulted Torrio and Capone's Sicilian heritage and bragged that he had outsmarted them.

On November 10, 1924, O'Banion was in the Chicago flower shop he operated as a front, making floral arrangements for

Despite the many illegal activities that the notorious Al Capone participated in—bootlegging, prostitution, and gang-style murders—he was eventually arrested for tax evasion.

the funeral of slain gangster Mike Merlo. Four men entered the shop and shot O'Banion dead at point-blank range. O'Banion's death, which had been ordered by Torrio and Capone, would not be the end of the killing.

"I Call Myself a Business Man"

Two of O'Banion's former henchmen, George "Bugs" Moran and Earl "Little Hymie" Weiss, continued to battle Capone for control of the Chicago rackets. In January 1925 Weiss and Moran ambushed Torrio, blasting him with shotguns. Moran was about to finish off the badly wounded Torrio with a pistol shot to the head but his weapon misfired. Just then police arrived. Torrio lived, but he was so badly shaken he left Chicago—putting the twenty-five-year-old Al Capone in charge of South Side rackets.

The bloodshed continued. At noon on September 20, 1926, ten carloads of Moran's gangsters slowly drove by Capone's headquarters. As they passed, they emptied thousands of rounds of machine-gun fire into the building. Capone fell to the floor unhurt. Miraculously, no one was killed.

Later that month Capone had his revenge when he arranged to have Hymie Weiss machine-gunned to death in front of Chicago's Holy Name Cathedral. The war ended on February 14, 1929—St. Valentine's Day—when seven of Bugs Moran's henchmen were machine-gunned at the garage that served as their headquarters. Moran was not among them, but the incident shattered his nerve. Capone was now the undisputed leader of Chicago rackets, catering to a thirsty public's desire

Prohibition agents Izzy Einstein (left) and Moe Smith were known for their ingenious enforcement methods.

for illegal booze. He expressed his point of view frankly:

> I make my money by satisfying a public demand. If I break the law, my customers, who number hundreds of the best people in Chicago, are as guilty as I am. The only difference between us is that I sell and they buy. Everybody calls me a racketeer. I call myself a business man. When I sell liquor, it's bootlegging. When my patrons serve it on a silver tray on Lake Shore Drive, it's hospitality.[20]

Izzy and Moe

Not all government officials were corrupt or lackadaisical regarding Prohibition. A few officials took their duties seriously—and worked hard to shut down speakeasies and arrest bootleggers. In New York City, a city that generally opposed Prohibition,

resided Isadore "Izzy" Einstein and Moe Smith, two of the nation's most industrious, and inventive, Prohibition agents. Neither looked like a typical federal agent. Einstein stood at just 5 feet, 5 inches and weighed 225 pounds; Smith was a couple of inches taller but weighed close to 300 pounds. Between 1920 and 1925 these two roly-poly agents were responsible for one-fifth of all the Prohibition arrests in Manhattan. The pair used numerous disguises, their mastery of foreign languages (Izzy could speak five languages fluently and three more with less skill), and an unbelievable amount of nerve.

Once Einstein walked into a speakeasy and wanted a drink. The bartender refused to sell alcohol to a stranger.

"Why, I'm Izzy Epstein, the famous Prohibition detective," Izzy responded.

The bartender didn't believe him—and pointed out the *real* detective was named *Einstein*—not *Ep*stein.

Alcohol Consumption

Drinking habits changed dramatically during and after Prohibition, as shown by these Census Bureau figures regarding the gallons of alcohol consumed per person during the years 1914 through 1940.

Year	Hard Liquor	Beer	Wine
1914 (only some local prohibition)	1.44	20.69	0.53
1918 (wartime federal prohibition)	0.85	14.87	0.48
1935 (one year after repeal of prohibition)	0.70	10.25	0.30
1940 (six years after repeal)	1.02	12.58	0.66

Izzy insisted it was *Ep*stein. "You're nuts!" the frustrated bartender shouted, "I'll bet you anything you want it's Einstein."

Izzy agreed. He'd bet for drinks. The bar's customers gathered around, looked at some newspaper accounts and decided it was Einstein. Izzy paid off—then promptly arrested the bartender for selling him the drinks.[21]

Some Were Dry

Yet despite widespread violations of the law, Prohibition was not a complete failure. Alcohol consumption dropped by 30 percent, particularly in the early 1920s. Even the U.S. Brewers' Association admitted that the consumption of hard liquor was off by 50 percent during Prohibition.

Even after Prohibition ended, hard liquor and beer consumption was dramatically lower than before Prohibition. "The amount of liquor consumption was reduced significantly during Prohibition," contends Jules Abels, author of *In the Time of Silent Cal*, "although drinking did continue on a massive scale."[22]

Many persons, however, gave up drinking entirely, not wishing to break the law or to associate with lawbreakers. In addition, changes in distribution patterns made necessary by the illegality of alcohol drove prices up, and booze became too expensive for those with modest incomes. Former drinkers now spent money on their families and homes. "In strictly economic terms, prohibition helped the poor people of America," writes historian Andrew Sinclair in *Era of Excess*. "The testimony of social workers is practically unanimous that during the first few years of the 'experiment, noble in motive,' the health and wealth of the workers of America increased and their drunkenness decreased."[23]

Chapter

3 A Controversial Decade: From Presidential Scandals to a Monkey Trial

During the '20s Americans disagreed furiously over several controversial court cases, including one over justice for foreign-born radicals accused of murder, and another over the death penalty in a case involving two wealthy teens who killed for a "thrill." The decade also witnessed the rise—and fall—of America's most famous hate group—the Ku Klux Klan. And a popular president was surrounded by political and personal scandals.

"There's a Bad Scandal Brewing"

On taking office in 1921, Warren Gamaliel Harding won public approval by appointing many highly qualified persons to his cabinet, including Secretary of Commerce Herbert Hoover, Secretary of the Treasury Andrew Mellon, and Secretary of Agriculture Henry Wallace. Harding praised these men as the "best minds." But the new president also appointed persons of highly questionable morality to public office. Indeed, the choices of two old cronies who were rewarded with cabinet posts turned out to be disastrous: Harry Daugherty was appointed attorney general and New Mexico senator Albert B. Fall secretary of the interior. Daugherty's selection was particularly controversial. He was clearly not a "best mind." The *New York Times* contended Harding had been content "to choose merely a best friend."[24]

To head the Veterans Administration, Harding selected Charles R. Forbes, who had been decorated for heroism in World War I. Forbes robbed the VA blind, taking bribes from contractors and selling off government assets at bargain-basement prices. When Harding found out about Forbes's misdeeds he forced him out of office, but

President Warren G. Harding poses with his vice president, Calvin Coolidge. During his administration, Harding made poor choices in some of his cabinet appointees.

the president's problems were only beginning. Daugherty had brought a close friend from Ohio, Jesse Smith, to Washington. Smith held no official government position but used his access to Daugherty to meddle to an extraordinary extent in the business of the Justice Department and to enrich himself illegally on many occasions. On May 30, 1923, Smith shot and killed himself in Daugherty's Washington apartment. Meanwhile Secretary of the Interior Fall was collecting $400,000 in bribes from those who wished to exploit the oil reserves on federal property at Teapot Dome, Wyoming, and Elk Hill, California. The Director of Alien Property Thomas W. Miller had received another $400,000 bribe to seize $7 million in German-owned property in the United States.

Harding Grows Suspicious

It took Harding a long time to become suspicious of his friends, whether out of naivete or ignorance, no one is sure. He worried mightily over their betrayal of his confidence. "I can take care of my enemies all right," he muttered. "But my damn friends, my God-damn-friends, . . . they're the ones that keep me walking the floor nights." [25]

In June 1923 Harding, worried about what his associates were up to, set out on a visit to the West Coast and Alaska to bolster public support for his "Normalcy" program of lower income taxes and government spending but higher tariffs. Crowds cheered the handsome president, enthusiastically receiving his proposals for a "return to normalcy," but Harding seemed tired and weak. Distressed by thoughts of how his friends had betrayed him, he summoned his secretary of commerce, Herbert Hoover. "Mr. Secretary," he said, "there's a bad scandal brewing in the administration. What do you think I should do? Keep it under cover or open it up?" When Hoover told him he should "open it up completely and without delay," a depressed-looking Harding did not re-

President Harding with his wife in 1921. Surrounded by scandal, Harding died of a heart attack before finishing out his term.

spond.[26] The strain became too much for him, and he died of a heart attack in San Francisco on August 2.

The nation mourned, but it would soon discover what the late president's friends had been plotting. Fall and Daugherty were forced from office (Fall, Charles Forbes, and Thomas W. Miller would later go to prison; Daugherty—who would refuse to testify on grounds of self-incrimination—would be acquitted of criminal charges). Harding himself did not appear to have been personally corrupt, but his reputation eroded disastrously as one scandal after another was revealed.

"Harding does not seem to have been involved in the actual misdemeanors of [his untrustworthy friends]" notes his biographer Andrew Sinclair. "The truth of the matter was probably best described by the Boston manager of the Hearst newspapers. He said Harding was made a fool of."[27]

Harding, however, was involved in other scandals that cheapened the reputation of the presidency. He and his cronies played poker in the White House, and even though Prohibition was in force, indulged in bootleg booze. Worse, marital infidelities were revealed. In Marion, Ohio, before becoming president, Harding had carried on an affair with a neighbor, Mrs. Carrie Phillips. Many people in Ohio knew of the relationship, but after Harding's nomination for the presidency, his supporters gave Mrs. Phillips and her husband a trip to Europe to get them out of the country for the duration of the campaign. Even while Harding was president he continued a relationship with Nan Britton that had begun in 1910 when Britton was just fourteen years old. She had a daughter by him in 1919.

When these facts became known with the publication of Nan Britton's *The Presi-dent's Daughter*—coupled with the actions of Harding's widow, who had both refused to allow an autopsy and burned the president's papers—all sorts of baseless rumors spread. Many believed that Harding had not died of natural causes. People even suspected Mrs. Harding of having poisoned her husband to protect him from having to face the scandals that would soon be uncovered, inevitably tarnishing his administration. Some believed their president had committed suicide.

The Monkey Trial

While scandals rocked the presidency and Prohibition laws were flouted right and left, there remained a segment of the population committed to the ideal of morality in every phase of the nation's life. Christian fundamentalists carried the battle over public morals and who should teach this battle into the public schools in a movement that resulted in the landmark trial of Tennessee biology teacher John T. Scopes.

In the nineteenth century, British naturalist Charles Darwin developed the theory according to which man and other species had gradually evolved from lower forms of life. Fundamentalists, people who believe in the literal truth of the Bible, felt that Darwin's theory was an attack on the biblical account of Creation, and some state legislatures passed laws prohibiting the teaching of evolution in public schools. Tennessee, Oklahoma, and Mississippi, where Fundamentalists were very influential, had such laws on their books.

The Tennessee legislature banned the teaching of any nonbiblical theory of human origins: "any theory that denies the

Lawyer Clarence Darrow (right) poses with client John T. Scopes (center) during the famous monkey trial. Scopes was brought to trial for teaching evolution.

Scopes's trial became a national sensation, popularly known as the monkey trial. Huge crowds of curiosity seekers thronged Dayton's courthouse. Rural evangelists set up revival tent meetings in the town. Over a hundred reporters from across the nation arrived. Western Union hired twenty-two telegraph operators to relay their news stories back to waiting editors. Radio stations broadcast live reports.

Darrow Faces Bryan

Much of the public's interest centered on the opposing lawyers in the case. Clarence Darrow, perhaps America's foremost defense attorney, headed John Scopes's team. William Jennings Bryan, three-time presidential candidate and Woodrow Wilson's secretary of state, journeyed to Tennessee to lead prosecution efforts. Both men were famous for their speaking ability. Darrow had successfully defended many prominent persons; Bryan, "the Silver-Tongued Orator of the Platte," had long been a hero to many in the West and South. A terrific battle was shaping up.

Scopes was clearly guilty of violating the law. Darrow never contested that point. Instead, he argued that the statute violated the constitutional principle of separation of church and state by forbidding teachers in Tennessee's public schools to present scientific material that was interpreted by representatives of some churches as contrary to their religious beliefs.

The trial's climax came when prosecutor Bryan, himself a Fundamentalist, took the witness stand. Darrow, a skeptic in matters of religion, grilled Bryan mercilessly, particularly concerning a literal interpre-

story of the Divine creation of man as taught in the Bible, and to teach instead that man has descended from a lower order of animals"[28]—on March 25, 1925. This meant that no science teacher in the state could discuss Darwin's theory. Many felt that this law and others like it were an assault on academic and intellectual freedom and the principle of separation of church and state. Thus, a number of Tennessee residents decided to challenge the 1925 law. This required having a teacher deliberately disobey the state law; the arrest of the volunteer would result in a trial, which would lead to a ruling on the constitutionality of the law. A Dayton, Tennessee, biology teacher named John T. Scopes was recruited for the test case.

tation of the Bible. Darrow showed that the biblical accounts of a whale that swallowed a man, a human general making the sun stand still at the Battle of Jericho, or God's creation of the earth in "six days of twenty-four hours"[29] could well be interpreted in metaphorical terms for spiritual purposes but were less easy for people with access to modern scientific knowledge to regard as literally.

Darrow attempted to discredit Fundamentalism in general, and Bryan personally. Bryan was just as determined to prevent the position Darrow was defending from gaining acceptance by the courts. Darrow bragged that he had vowed "to show up Fundamentalism . . . to prevent bigots and ignoramuses from controlling the educational system of the United States." Bryan

Attorney William Jennings Bryan, "the Silver-Tongued Orator of the Platte," was the prosecutor during the Scopes trial.

shot back that he was fighting "to protect the word of God against the greatest atheist and agnostic in the United States!"[30]

The court found John Scopes guilty and fined him $100, but in the larger court of public opinion his cause won. Bryan's view of the world—that every word of the Bible should be taken literally—was widely ridiculed by reporters and commentators. Five days after the trial ended, Bryan died of a stroke. Many believed that along with the sweltering heat of a Tennessee summer and the poor physical condition of an older, overweight man, the humiliation of Darrow's attacks on Bryan's intellect had brought on the fatal stroke.

Scopes appealed to the Tennessee Supreme Court. That court declined to overturn the antievolution law but nonetheless reversed Scopes's conviction—on the grounds that his $100 fine had been excessive.

The Thrill Killing

The public of the Roaring Twenties also followed the sensational murder trial of two young "thrill killers." On May 21, 1924, nineteen-year-old Nathan Leopold Jr. and eighteen-year-old Richard Loeb kidnapped and murdered fourteen-year-old Bobby Franks. The young men's reason for the killing was unusual. Leopold and Loeb, whose families together were worth $15 million, believed that they were mental and social giants, above the common herd. They had plotted to commit "the perfect murder" for a "thrill," just to prove how smart they were. They even callously planned to swindle the younger boy's grieving family out of a $10,000 ransom.

Less brilliant than they had imagined, Leopold and Loeb made numerous blunders and were caught almost immediately. On the advice of their attorney, Clarence Darrow, they entered guilty pleas. Then for three days the famous lawyer worked to save them from the electric chair, arguing against the death penalty, telling the jury that killing these two young men would accomplish nothing. It would not solve the world's problems, but would only increase its cruelty and hatred. Darrow's eloquence,

"Mr. Bryan's Private Affair"

The New York World *sympathized with Clarence Darrow's position in the Scopes trial at Dayton, Tennessee, but found itself uneasy as Darrow baited prosecuting attorney William Jennings Bryan on the witness stand. James Boylan's* The World and the 20s *reprints the* World*'s editorial of July 25, 1925.*

"Just because The World believes that there is a serious issue underlying the Dayton trial it has no sympathy at all for the manner in which Mr. Darrow heckled Mr. Bryan. The attempt to prove as part of the legal record that Mr. Bryan is ignorant of many things has nothing to do with the case. When Mr. Bryan said 'I have all the information I want to live by and die by;' when he said 'I believe in creation as there [in the Bible] told, and if I am not able to explain it I will accept it,' he was announcing a faith for which he is not accountable in any court of law, nor fairly subject to ridicule at the bar of public opinion.

The only question is whether Mr. Bryan shall be permitted to establish his religion officially in the State of Tennessee. It does not matter whether it is a true religion or a false religion; it does not matter whether Mr. Bryan is ignorant or learned. The only question is whether he shall be allowed to call out the police. Mr. Darrow achieves nothing but obfuscation when he makes it appear that Mr. Bryan's campaign would be less objectionable if Mr. Bryan had read more books and took a more sophisticated view of the Bible. . . .

Mr. Darrow has no right to attack Mr. Bryan's religion. That is wholly Mr. Bryan's private affair. What is legitimately an object of attack is the effort of Mr. Bryan to impose his religion upon the Government of a State. It is upon the pretension to use the Government for a sectarian purpose that the champions of religious liberty should concentrate their fire."

The sons of millionaires, Richard Loeb and Nathan Leopold confessed to slaying fourteen-year-old Bobby Franks in their attempt to commit the perfect crime.

for which he was paid $300,000, saved his clients from the electric chair. Instead of the death penalty they received life plus 99 years. In 1936 Loeb was murdered in prison. Leopold was paroled in 1958.

Red Scare

Throughout the decade, while criminal trials captured and fueled the public's imagination, Americans were concerned about other law-and-order issues as well. Disruptive strikes swept the nation: police officers in Boston and radicals in Seattle were among the groups staging serious work actions. Workers struck to protest low wages (the Boston police were particularly low paid), long hours (particularly for women and children), and often dangerous working conditions. Some workers believed the entire political system of the United States was to blame for their treatment. Many participated in organized groups that adhered to the concept of socialism, and some were members of the Communist Party. In 1917 V. I. Lenin and the Bolsheviks (communists) had seized power in Russia. Communists then tried to bring down the governments of Germany and Hungary. Although the last two attempted coups failed, many feared that revolutionaries in the United States would try to imitate Lenin and overthrow the capitalist system, as he had put an end to czarism in Russia. Prejudices were inflamed because some of the most highly visible radicals were foreign born.

The fear grew that law and order was breaking down. In response, in 1919–1920, Attorney General A. Mitchell Palmer (whose own home was damaged by a leftist's bomb) ordered numerous headquarters for organizations and private homes raided in search of radicals whom he charged with conspiracy to overthrow the government. Over six thousand men and women were arrested in these "Palmer raids"—some were deported to Russia, but most were freed. Many suspected that Palmer, who unsuccessfully sought the Democratic nomination in 1920, was motivated more by presidential ambitions than by a concern to protect the government from violent overthrow.

Sacco and Vanzetti

Many people today, as in the twenties, believed the fear of radicalism drove the prosecution of a very ordinary—but bloody—crime. On April 15, 1920, five men robbed a shoe factory in South Braintree, Massachusetts. While getting away with $15,776.51 they killed the company paymaster and a factory guard.

Twenty days later police in nearby Brockton arrested two Italian immigrants for handing out anarchist pamphlets on a street corner. Soon shoemaker Nicola Sacco and fish peddler Bartolomeo Vanzetti were charged with committing the South Braintree robbery and murders as well. Before the pair was tried for the shoe factory shoot out, Vanzetti, who had been accused of participating in an earlier robbery, was found guilty on that charge.

By the time Sacco and Vanzetti were brought to trial for the South Braintree murders, the case was attracting a great deal of attention. Many radicals and liberals thought that the arrests of the two immigrants had more to do with their background and political beliefs than with

Attorney General A. Mitchell Palmer staged raids on private homes and organizations in attempts to uncover political radicals.

evidence. The small but active U.S. Communist Party was especially interested in the case and sent a lawyer to assist in the defense of the two immigrants. The strongest evidence against Vanzetti came from his own .32-caliber Colt pistol. A prosecution ballistics expert linked the weapon to the bullets that had killed the factory guard, Alessandro Berardelli. But defense experts claimed the evidence was inconclusive. The weapon also caused Vanzetti trouble when he admitted he had lied to police about how long he had owned it. In July 1921 both men were found guilty and sentenced to death by Judge Webster Thayer.

Sacco and Vanzetti's conviction served to renew the controversy. Questions were raised as to whether they had been railroaded because of their radical politics and foreign origins. Judge Thayer, for example, had allegedly sworn to "get those bastards [Sacco and Vanzetti] good and proper."[31] European and South American newspapers seemed particularly fascinated, and in France crowds rioted at demonstrations on Sacco and Vanzetti's behalf. Elsewhere, bombs exploded at American embassies. Back in America, intellectuals, impressed by the defendants' quiet dignity, rose to support them. "The men in Charleston prison are shining spirits," wrote newspaperman Heywood Hale Broun. "They are too bright, we shield our eyes and kill them. We are the dead, and in us there is not feeling nor imagination nor the terrible torment of lust for justice."[32]

Massachusetts governor Alvan Fuller appointed a panel to look into the case, but this group reported finding the jury's verdict to be justified and urged Fuller not to pardon the defendants. On August 23, 1927, Nicola Sacco and Bartolomeo Vanzetti were electrocuted at Dedham Prison. Shortly thereafter a bomb exploded at Judge Thayer's home. Sacco and Vanzetti were dead but not forgotten by their many defenders.

The Ku Klux Klan

While liberals and radicals rallied around Sacco and Vanzetti at least partly because they were anarchist immigrants, other Americans were just as eager to believe the two were *guilty* because they were anarchist immigrants. Many Protestant, Anglo-Saxon Americans feared the large number of Catholic and Jewish immigrants from southern and eastern Europe. Many also

Nicola Sacco and Bartolomeo Vanzetti arrive at the courthouse during their trial. Even today people debate whether the two immigrants were guilty of murder.

wanted to keep black Americans from advancing and competing with whites. In the 1920s those who most passionately opposed Catholics, Jews, and blacks joined the white-robed legions of the Ku Klux Klan. The Klan became an immensely powerful political force, numbering millions of members. But it was involved in more than politics. It spread fear and dread wherever it went, often torturing and murdering its victims.

The Ku Klux Klan was not a new idea. These domestic terrorists first organized after the Civil War, to help southerners resist Reconstruction, the federal occupation of those states that had tried to secede. When the victorious northerners left the South, the KKK faded away, but in 1915 a

"The Systematic Sale of Race Hatred"

The New York World *was the first to expose the activities of the Ku Klux Klan. This excerpt from the* World's *September 6, 1921, issue, quoted in James Boylan's* The World and the 20s, *discusses just how lucrative a Klan organizer's job could be.*

"This [Klan membership] drive is being actively pushed in scores of communities throughout the United States. The Kleagles [Klan recruiters] collect no initiation fees, but each new member makes a 'donation' of $10, of which the Kleagle keeps $4 and sends the rest to his King Kleagle [head of the Klan in each state or 'realm'], who pockets another $1. The remaining $5 vanishes into the 'imperial' treasury of the order.

Furthermore, the Klan itself owns the company manufacturing the regalia of cotton robe and hooded cap, which is sold to members for $6.50 and costs $1.25 to make. The whole 'propagation' department is in the hands of professional drive leaders, whose sole interest in Ku Kluxism is in the 'split' just outlined.

In the last five years membership 'donations' and sales of regalia have yielded at least $5,000,000—probably a considerably greater sum. Ku Kluxing from the inside has been a paying enterprise and its lucrative possibilities have recently been increased by the decision to admit women as well as men to membership. The sisters can now come in with the brothers at only $10 per come-on.

The original Knights of the Ku Klux Klan, Inc., modestly begun five years ago, has become a vast enterprise, doing a thriving business in the systematic sale of race hatred, religious bigotry and '100 per cent' anti-Americanism."

Georgian, Colonel William Joseph Simmons, revived the Klan as a secret white supremacist fraternal order.

Simmons seems to have had very modest goals for his organization. In 1920, however, Edward Y. Clark, a public relations specialist, joined the group. Thanks to Clark the organization grew rapidly. Unlike the original Klan, this new KKK had a much bigger list of enemies. Besides blacks, Klansmen of the 1920s directed their violent acts of intimidation against Roman Catholics (particularly foreign-born Catholics) and Jews. "These old stock Americans are coming to believe that the Jews dominate the economic life of the nation," wrote one Klan leader in the KKK's newspaper *Fiery Cross*, "while the Catholics are determined to dominate the political and religious life. And they have apprehensions that the vast alien immigration is at root an attack upon Protestant religion with its freedom of conscience, and is therefore a menace to American liberties."[33] The Klan also devoted time to harassing bootleggers and those suspected of acts of sexual immorality.

Terrorist Acts

The Klan did not restrict itself to mere words. It continued in the terrorist tradition of the nineteenth-century group. Its anonymous, hooded members spread fear nationwide, burning crosses, and lynching, whipping, and tarring and feathering victims who included blacks, Catholics, Jews, radicals, and bootleggers. The Klan was responsible for over a thousand assaults in Texas and Oklahoma, at least a hundred each in Georgia, Florida, and Alabama and dozens more in other states. One of the worst outrages occurred in Morehouse Parish, Louisiana, where two white men who had criticized the Klan were kidnapped on August 24, 1922. They were then flogged and run over by a road grader. Their bodies were dismembered and thrown into Lake Lafourche. Even though over fifty witnesses took the stand in two separate grand jury investigations, no one was ever held responsible for the crime. Early Klan leaders encouraged violence and brutality. "There are a lot of fellows who come to me . . . and want just a little of the rough stuff,"[34] Edward Y. Clark once bragged about those who joined the KKK.

Despite—or perhaps because of—such talk of violence, the Klan grew rapidly under Clark's leadership. In July 1923 a hundred thousand hooded and robed members of the "invisible empire" gathered in Kokomo, Indiana. By 1924 the Klan had recruited 3 million members. In 1925 forty thousand Klansmen paraded down Washington's Pennsylvania Avenue. Klan political influence was huge—and not just in the South. Indiana, Oregon, Ohio, Maine, and Colorado had very active chapters. Even politicians who loathed the Klan feared it, not knowing just how many members the secret society counted in each election district, or even *who* those members might be. "Behind the Klan mask," wrote journalist and poet Robert Frost, "is a political power of unknown potency, and one that cannot be reached even for propitiation and bargaining unless it wishes to be reached."[35]

Yet Americans and even KKK members tired of the Klan's violence, bigotry, and lawlessness. They also were sickened by personal scandals involving top Klan leaders. In 1922 Simmons and Clark (who had

The Ku Klux Klan marches down Pennsylvania Avenue in 1925. The Klan both rose to prominence and fell from grace during the 1920s.

been accused of misusing Klan funds) were forced to resign. The Klan's new head, David C. Stephenson, helped elect the top leaders in Indiana state government and thought he could become president of the United States. His plans soon collapsed in 1925, however, when he was found guilty of murder following the death of a woman he had sexually attacked. Many disgusted Klan members resigned from the organization. "The godly," notes historian David Chalmers, "came to realize the Klan was not." [36]

The KKK fell as rapidly as it had risen. By 1930 its membership had shrunk to thirty thousand.

4 The Culture of the '20s: Silents, Talkies, and All That Jazz

During the 1920s opportunities for culture and entertainment were increasingly available to the average American. The invention of radio brought a tremendous sense of excitement to American homes. Since Shakespeare's day—indeed, since the days of Greek tragedies and Roman circuses—people had had to leave their houses and travel to theaters, concert halls, or circuses to enjoy live performances. Now they could stay at home and enjoy broadcast music, drama, and comedy. This was particularly amazing to those living in small cities or remote farms, now able to hear the same headline acts that had once been accessible only in big cities. A new world opened up, and Americans flocked to stores to buy primitive radios, rushing home to fiddle with antennas and dials in an often frustrating, exciting struggle to receive a decent signal.

Today, listening to a radio involves making a small purchase, plugging the radio in or inserting batteries, and turning

Listeners enjoy an early radio, called a crystal set, in the early 1920s. Unfortunately, crystal radios were very difficult to operate.

on the sound. Early radios, however, were expensive (in 1926 a Freshman model radio cost $150) and very difficult to operate. The first commercially made radios were called crystal sets and needed headphones. Even when radios moved past the crystal set stage, they required two different batteries for operation. An "A" battery had to be recharged every two weeks. A "B" battery had to be replaced every two to three weeks. Not until 1927 was it possible to simply plug a radio into normal house current. Reception was also difficult, and listeners had to string hundred-foot wire antennas outside their houses. Even then, crackling static, caused by moisture in the atmosphere, often ruined reception.

Radio Firsts

Not that there was much to listen to at first. Early stations were often operated for public relations purposes by manufacturers, newspapers, department stores—or even amateur radio enthusiasts. The earliest stations included WWJ in Detroit, WGY in Schenectady, New York, and KDKA in Pittsburgh. There was little regulation of frequencies or of broadcasting power. Not until 1927 would the federal government formally assign frequencies to competing radio stations.

Radio sales increased dramatically throughout the '20s. In 1922 only 3 million American homes boasted radios, and sales amounted to just $60 million. By 1929 that figure increased to $852 million. As the decade drew to a close, 10 million homes, 5 million businesses, and 2 million cars featured radio sets.

At first few believed radio could be used to advertise products. "Any attempt," one advertising trade journal admitted in 1922, "to make the radio an advertising medium would, we think, prove positively offensive to great numbers of people."[37] Later that year, however, the first radio advertising appeared on New York station WEAF. The precedent-setting ad was much like the brief messages now broadcast on public TV and radio—just a mention that the program was made possible by a local real estate firm.

Quickly, however, advertising and programming became virtually inseparable. Advertisers sponsored the production of programs such as *The Eveready Hour*, or *Lux Soap Radio Theater*. Advertising was big business in the 1920s and helped spur sales of products of all sorts, from autos to cigarettes to appliances. By mid-decade $1.25 billion a year was being spent to advertise products—on radio, in newspapers, and in magazines.

Other radio firsts were also taking place. The first sports broadcast was an April 1921 lightweight boxing match, aired over KDKA in Pittsburgh. That same year, the Dempsey-Carpentier heavyweight title fight was broadcast, as was the first baseball game, a regular season Pirates-Phillies contest. Early entertainment shows included such now forgotten acts as the Happiness Boys, the Cliquot Club Eskimos, and the A&P Gypsies. By 1929 many of radio's most popular shows were on the air. *Amos 'n' Andy* portrayed the comic adventures of two African Americans. Crooner Rudy Vallee, fresh out of Yale University, invented the variety show format. Comedienne Gertrude Berg, star of *The Goldbergs*, developed a very early situation comedy.

The first radio stations were all run independently. Not until 1926 would the

(Left) An early broadcasting station in 1920 shows the station's entire staff: an engineer, an announcer, and two assistants. (Below) The huge, ornate Fox Theater in Detroit.

first network, the National Broadcasting Company (NBC) form. The Columbia Broadcasting System (CBS) followed a year later. Radio had become big business.

Silent Pictures

Radio talked, but motion pictures were silent. Movies had been mute since inventor Thomas Edison developed them in the 1890s. Despite the lack of sound, movies grew in popularity, bringing slapstick comedies and swashbuckling adventures to theater audiences. Movie attendance reached 20 million in 1922, and had doubled by 1929. Huge new theaters were built to hold the crowds that wanted to see the silent films. Detroit's Fox Theater and New York's Roxy—"the Cathedral of the Motion Picture"—each seated 5,000 patrons. New York's Capitol Theater was even larger, seating 5,300. These theaters were not just large, they were "movie palaces." The Roxy cost $10 million to build, featured three organs, wall-length paintings, and life-size statues. Its spectacular red carpet alone cost $100,000.

The theaters were big, and so were the stars that movies created. Performers such as one time ranch hand William S. Hart and former Kansas sheriff Tom Mix dominated the western; dashing Douglas Fairbanks specialized in adventure films such as *Robin Hood* (1922), *The Thief of Bagdad* (1924), and *The Mark of Zorro* (1925); and Francis X. Bushman and Ramon Novarro starred in the epic *Ben Hur* (1926). But

Roaring Twenties audiences loved comedies best of all. Three of the most popular comics in what critics later called the golden age of comedy were Charlie Chaplin, Buster Keaton, and Harold Lloyd.

Chaplin, originally an English music hall performer, had immigrated to the United States in 1913. Usually, he portrayed a character known as the Little Tramp. This forlorn character was a picture of tattered elegance. With a shabby derby hat, baggy pants, and an odd shuffling walk, Chaplin stole his way into the hearts of moviegoers in such classic films as *The Kid* (1921), *The Gold Rush* (1926), and *The Circus* (1926).

Buster Keaton got his laughs by employing a serious, deadpan expression. "If I laughed at what I did," he once explained, "the audience didn't. The more serious I turned, the bigger laugh I got."[38]

Two of Keaton's greatest films were *Sherlock, Jr.* (1923), in which he portrayed an amateur detective, and a Civil War comedy called *The General* (1927), which featured a classic high-speed train chase.

Chaplin and Keaton played outlandish, hardly believable characters, but Harold Lloyd prospered by portraying an average-looking, businesslike man who found himself in outlandish, hardly believable situations and quietly persevered. Often Lloyd would be seen hanging from buildings or performing all sorts of dangerous-looking stunts. "I symbolize the little struggling man working at a menial job," the actor once observed. "He might be a soda jerk, a ribbon salesman or somebody trying to get a job. In any event he was always struggling against the bigger man in a difficult situation."[39] A lot of little struggling men and women must have identified with Lloyd

Edna Purviance and Charlie Chaplin star in the silent film Work. *Chaplin was known for his character the Little Tramp.*

Rudolph Valentino stars in Son of the Sheik. *Valentino was a 1920s heartthrob, playing sexy, romantic, and exotic characters.*

and gone to see his films. As early as 1920 he was earning $1 million per year and living in a multimillion-dollar home.

The Sheik

The greatest star of the twenties, however, was not a comedian. It was exotic leading man Rudolph Valentino. Motion pictures had already created such action stars as Douglas Fairbanks, but the dark-featured Valentino added a broad hint of dangerous sensuality to his performances.

Valentino (his real name was Rodolpho d'Antonguella) came to the United States in 1913 from Italy. Ironically, in a decade remembered for its hostility to foreigners, many of its most awesome film stars—Valentino, Chaplin, Novarro, and actress Pola Negri—were foreign born, while sultry Cincinnati native Theda Bara pretended to be. Valentino's performance in the 1921 film *The Four Horsemen of the Apocalypse* catapulted him to stardom. His next film, *The Sheik*, cemented his fame. Audiences, particularly female audience members, saw Valentino as sexy. "With his sideburns and his passionate air," notes historian Frederick Lewis Allen in *Only Yesterday*, "the Sheik had set the standard for masculine sex appeal." [40] Later films such as *Blood and Sand* (1922), in which he starred as a bullfighter, *Monsieur Beaucaire* (1924), *The Eagle* (1925), and *Son of the Sheik* (1926) only increased Valentino's popularity.

But like James Dean, Marilyn Monroe, and Kurt Cobain, Valentino died young. He suffered a burst appendix in August 1926 and was dead at the age of thirty-one.

"A Vast and Dizzy Success"

H. L. Mencken met silent film star Rudolph Valentino just a few weeks before the actor's death. In this excerpt from an article that appeared in the August 26, 1926, issue of the Baltimore Evening Sun *(quoted in Alistair Cooke's* The Vintage Mencken*), the journalist identifies Valentino, despite his fame and wealth, as a very unhappy young person.*

"Had he achieved, out of nothing, a vast and dizzy success? Then that success was as hollow as it was vast—a colossal and preposterous nothing. Was he acclaimed by yelling multitudes? Then every time the multitudes yelled he was blushing inside. . . . Valentino was only the hero of the rabble. Imbeciles surrounded him in a dense herd. He was pursued by women—but what women! . . . The thing, at the start, must have only bewildered him. But in those last days, unless I am a worse psychologist than even those professors of psychology, it was revolting him. Worse, it was making him afraid. . . .

Here was a young man who was living daily the dream of millions of other young men. Here was one who was catnip to women. Here was one who had wealth and fame. And here was one who was very unhappy."

Rudolph Valentino died at age thirty-one from a burst appendix.

The Sheik's funeral was spectacular, outdoing even those of Chicago gangsters. A hundred thousand grief-stricken (or just curious) persons filed past his coffin. Fifty thousand mourners attended the funeral. Several women committed suicide. Little did they know that not long after the death of the great star, the medium that made him famous, the silent film, would also cease to be.

The Talkies

Inventor Lee DeForest had demonstrated a method of adding sound to movies as early as 1923, but motion picture studios were in no rush to embrace the new technology. For starters, sound equipment was very expensive. In addition, there was no guarantee that all the studios' silent stars would successfully make the conversion to talking films. And 40 percent of Hollywood's revenues came from foreign audiences. Making films with English-language dialogue could hurt sales abroad.

All that changed on October 6, 1927, when the nearly bankrupt Warner Brothers studio took a desperate chance and released *The Jazz Singer*, starring popular entertainer Al Jolson. *The Jazz Singer* was not a true sound film. There is some spoken dialogue and some singing by Jolson, but the rest of the feature was produced in the conventional (silent) mode. Yet *The Jazz Singer* created a sensation and soon doomed the silent film.

In many early talkies the gimmick of sound overshadowed everything else as scripts called for actors to blather on and on simply to showcase the novelty of talking.

A 1927 photograph shows the Warners' Theatre marquis during the premier of The Jazz Singer, *the movie that marked the start of the talkie and the demise of the silent film.*

"Mr. Jolson's First Picture"

The 1927 film The Jazz Singer *introduced sound to movies and changed Hollywood. This is what the October 17, 1927, issue of* Time *magazine had to say about the movie.*

"Two seasons ago Manhattan and other cities witnessed approvingly the theatrical tale of a Jewish boy who wanted to go on the stage. . . . His . . . father [who followed the Orthodox tradition] fumed gently, having trained him for a cantor. But circumstance and the boy's yearning for the footlights made him in the end a singer of jazz for the world that lives at night. George Jessel, a jazz singer from revue and vaudeville, played the part and made his name as a straight actor. But in making the picture Mr. Jessel was passed over in favor of the man whom so many worship as their greatest entertainer, Al Jolson. It is Mr. Jolson's first picture and as such of great import to the history of the current theatre. In no other way but pictures can his genius be preserved; and in this he is favored with the double preservative of picture and mechanical voice reproduction. The Vitaphone permits him to talk and sing his way through the sentimental mazes of the movie adaptation. He is a good actor; but he is a very great singer of popular songs. In cities where the Vitaphone can be installed and reproduce his voice this picture will eminently repay attendance."

Al Jolson was propelled to instant fame when he starred in the first talking movie, The Jazz Singer.

F. Scott Fitzgerald and his wife, Zelda, peer out from their automobile during their honeymoon. Novelist Fitzgerald's books portrayed the lives of the wealthy.

"Camera movement stopped," note film historians George N. Fenin and William K. Everson in *The Western*. "Plot stopped, action stopped, while the characters stood around and talked at length."[41]

By early 1929 two thousand of the nation's fifteen thousand movie theaters had converted to sound. The change ruined the careers of stars who were now unsuited for movie work. Leading man John Gilbert's voice was too high, for example. Polish-born Pola Negri could barely speak English. But dramatic actor John Barrymore survived, and Hollywood created new stars, importing talent from Broadway, where actors and actresses had never stopped talking.

The Written Word

Despite the new technologies of radio and talking pictures, the American public still found plenty of time to read.

The Roaring Twenties produced a number of significant authors. Novelist F. Scott Fitzgerald chronicled the high living of the era in *The Great Gatsby* (1925). Sinclair Lewis, on the other hand, critically portrayed the middle class and small town America, with all its faults. For novels such as *Main Street* (1920), *Babbitt* (1922), and *Elmer Gantry* (1927), he won the Nobel Prize in literature in 1930. Magazine editors H. L. Mencken and George Jean Nathan savagely ridiculed the American middle class or bourgeoisie (Mencken mocked them as the "booboisie"), first with the *Smart Set* magazine, then after 1925 with a new publication, the *American Mercury*.

In New York City, a circle of writers gathered for lunch each day at the Algonquin Hotel. Members included playwrights George S. Kaufman and Edna Ferber, poet and critic Dorothy Parker, humorist Robert Benchley, columnists Franklin Pierce Adams and Heywood Broun, and writer Alexander Woollcott. The wisecracks and cynical witticisms of the so-called Algonquin circle were often reported in the daily press. Typical of their wit was a remark by Dorothy Parker: Informed that playwright Clare Booth Luce was always kind to her inferiors, Parker, who did not care for Luce, responded, "And where does she find them?"[42]

The Marx brothers, (left to right) Zeppo, Groucho, Chico, and Harpo, star in The Cocoanuts. *The brothers became movie stars after spending years performing in vaudeville and Broadway shows.*

In the daily newspapers, people wanted to read about all the fads, foolishness, and scandals that marked the times. A young New York reporter named Walter Winchell developed the first gossip column. In 1919 a new form of newspaper—the tabloid—debuted. Tabloid pages were smaller than those of regular newspapers, but the main difference between the two forms of journalism lay in how they covered stories and what events they chose to feature. Tabloids specialize in human-interest stories and sensationalism. The most colorful tabloid of all was the *New York Graphic*, whose features included "Composographs," or composite or

faked photos of celebrities, and articles on contests, murders, and romantic serials. Other tabloids were not nearly as wild but, nonetheless, they had no trouble filling their pages with the scandals and sensations of the decade.

The Great White Way

Although the '20s saw the introduction of important new media, an older form of entertainment, stage plays as presented on New York City's Broadway, flourished as well. In addition, in the Roaring Twenties Broadway discovered one of the wildest acts ever to hit show business—the Marx Brothers.

The Marxes—wisecracking Groucho, silent Harpo, piano-playing Chico, and straight man Zeppo—had long toured vaudeville, but in 1922 they became Broadway sensations in *I'll Say She Is.* They followed up their initial success with two more madcap hits, *The Cocoanuts* (a spoof of the Florida land boom) and *Animal Crackers.*

Even more popular than the Marx Brothers, however, was *Abie's Irish Rose,* a comedy about an Irish girl who marries a Jewish boy. The critics hated it because of its lack of intelligence and humor, but it ran for a then-record 2,327 performances. "Where do people come from who keep

---

"Why Should One Speak?"

No show business act was more popular than the Four Marx Brothers, first on Broadway and later in the movies. When the review I'll Say She Is *opened on Broadway in 1924, the New York* World*'s critic Alexander Woollcott (as quoted in Groucho Marx and Richard J. Anobile's* The Marx Brothers Scrapbook) *welcomed the brothers enthusiastically.*

"As one of many who laughed immodestly throughout the greater part of the first performance given by the new musical show, entitled, if memory serves, "I'll Say She Is," it behooves your correspondent to report the most comical moments vouchsafed [given as presents] to the first nighters in a month of Mondays. It is a brightly colored and vehement setting for the goings on of those talented cutups, the Four Marx Brothers. In particular, it is a splendacious and reasonably tuneful excuse for going to see that silent brother, that shy, unexpected, magnificent comic among the Marxes, who is recorded somewhere on a birth certificate as Arthur, but who is known to the adoring . . . as Harpo Marx.

Surely there should be dancing in the streets when a great clown comic comes to town, and this man is a great clown. He is officially billed as a member of the Marx family, but truly he belongs to that greater family which includes Joe Jackson and Bert Melrose and the Fratlilni brothers, who fall over one another in so obliging a fashion at the Cirque Medrano in Paris. Harpo Marx, so styled, oddly enough because he plays the harp, says never a word from first to last, but when by merely leaning against one's brother can seem richly and irresistibly amusing why should one speak?"

---

this going?" wrote a puzzled *Life* reviewer, Robert Benchley. "You don't see them out in the daytime."[43]

Also popular on Broadway were producer Florenz "Flo" Ziegfeld's reviews. Reviews were not plays but lavish patchworks of musical and comedy numbers. Each year the producer would stage another edition of his Ziegfeld Follies. The shows featured scantily clad showgirls—"glorifying the American girl" is how Ziegfeld described his presentations—and many big-name comedians such as W. C. Fields, Fannie Brice, Will Rogers, and Eddie Cantor.

But Broadway also had a serious side, and some of the finest theatrical writing ever done in America was introduced on Broadway in the 1920s. Eugene O'Neill's

Beyond the Horizon (1920); *Anna Christie* (1922), the story of a prostitute's struggle for redemption; and *Strange Interlude* (1928), a psychological study of a woman, all won Pulitzer Prizes.

Slowly African Americans were beginning to appear on Broadway. Eugene O'Neill's drama *The Emperor Jones*, about a black Pullman porter who becomes dictator of a tropical island, was produced in 1922. African American Paul Robeson, a former football star at Rutgers and graduate of Columbia Law School, was an extremely popular performer during the Roaring Twenties. His deep bass voice thrilled audiences in such hit shows as *Show Boat* (in which he introduced "Ol' Man River") and *Porgy and Bess*, as well as in numerous concerts.

The Jazz Age

Singer Paul Robeson, a popular performer during the Roaring Twenties, would later become controversial for his political views.

Paul Robeson was not the only famous black entertainer of the 1920s. New styles of music emerged during the decade. Jazz, the most important, was developed by black musicians in the South. Starting in 1917, however, other Americans became aware of this lively musical form. Jazz spread from New Orleans to Kansas City to Chicago to New York.

Among the most famous black jazz musicians were trumpet player Louis Armstrong, singer Bessie Smith, and pianist-composer-bandleader Duke Ellington. Armstrong, who had grown up in a New Orleans reformatory, joined King Oliver's popular Chicago-based Creole Jazz Band in 1922, and his spirited playing made him a rising musical star. Bessie Smith, who also had a background of poverty, became

The Cotton Club in New York City was the jazz mecca of the 1920s. Duke Ellington, Cab Calloway, and other jazz greats made their start at this club.

known as the Empress of the Blues. Her first recording, "Down Hearted Blues" (released in 1923), sold over 2 million copies. Duke Ellington started his own band in Washington in 1918 and by 1923 was a successful pianist and bandleader.

African American culture flourished in New York's Harlem. Its most famous nightclub was the Cotton Club, which opened for business in 1927. Radio broadcasts of Ellington's performances helped create the Cotton Club's phenomenal popularity.

Soon white dance bands, such as those conducted by Paul Whiteman, Guy Lombardo, and Fred Waring were playing watered-down, strictly arranged versions of the high-energy, daringly improvisational music of the black jazz performers.

It was not until the night of February 12, 1924, however, that jazz truly became respectable. On that date, at New York's Aeolian Hall, Paul Whiteman's orchestra offered the first performance of twenty-five-year-old composer George Gershwin's *Rhapsody in Blue*, the first major symphonic work to use the jazz form. It was no ordinary jazz performance. In the audience were such classical music greats as violinist Jascha Heifitz and composers Igor Stravinsky, Sergey Rachmaninoff, and Victor Herbert. They liked what they heard—and so did the public. Jazz was here to stay.

5 The Golden Age of Sports

Americans have long loved sports. The first American professional sports team, baseball's Cincinnati Red Stockings, debuted in 1869. At the turn of the century, boxers such as John L. Sullivan and the black champion Jack Johnson were major public figures. So were baseball players Honus Wagner, Christy Mathewson, and Ty Cobb. Traditionally, baseball had been America's favorite sport, and baseball players its favorite athletes. Indeed, baseball was called the national pastime. But it was not until the Roaring Twenties that sports became big business and a new generation of athletes arose to capture the American imagination.

"Say It Ain't So, Joe"

The '20s began, however, with a shocking sports scandal. In September 1920 rumors spread that the 1919 World Series—in which the favored Chicago White Sox had been defeated by the Cincinnati Reds—had been fixed. There were increasingly credible reports that gamblers had bribed several Chicago players to play to lose. Soon such White Sox stars as outfielders Shoeless Joe Jackson and Happy Felsch as well as pitchers Eddie Cicotte and Lefty

Williams confessed to participating in the fix. The news rocked public confidence in idolized baseball players. Young fans were especially shocked. They *wanted* to believe in baseball and its heroes. "Say it ain't so, Joe,"[44] one youngster begged Jackson.

The Black Sox—as the crooked White Sox players were now known—went to trial. Despite massive evidence of their guilt they were acquitted by a jury. Many suspected the jury had been bribed; the jurors and defendants, for example, celebrated together after the verdict. The defendants' confessions had been stolen from the state attorney's office. The public grew more disenchanted.

But team owners recognized the need to restore public confidence in their tarnished game. Thus they created the office of baseball commissioner, a position that exists today. To this job they appointed a white-haired federal judge named Kenesaw Mountain Landis. Landis was known for his honesty and his toughness, and he expelled the officially exonerated players with these words:

> Regardless of the verdict of juries, no player that throws a ball game; no player that undertakes or promises to throw a ball game; no player that sits in a conference with a bunch of crooked

(Left) Judge Kenesaw Mountain Landis (center) was appointed baseball commissioner because of his no-nonsense, honest image. (Below) Babe Ruth was as well known for his incredible talent in baseball as he was for his notoriously ribald lifestyle.

players and gamblers where the ways and means of throwing games are planned and discussed and does not promptly tell his club about it, will ever play professional baseball.[45]

The words—and tough actions—of Judge Landis paved the way for Americans to once again believe in their athletic heroes.

The Sultan of Swat

The first baseball commissioner did not restore baseball's popularity single-handedly. Kenesaw Mountain Landis had help from the most popular and beloved athlete in the history of sports, George Herman "Babe" Ruth. Babe Ruth did not talk about the integrity of the game—or much else. He let his bat do his talking, and his powerful hitting made fans forget about the Black Sox.

Ruth's father was a Baltimore saloon keeper, and young George ran wild as a child. Unable to control his son, Ruth senior committed the boy to a local Catholic orphanage. There he learned to play baseball and signed a contract with Baltimore's

minor league team. In 1914 Ruth, then a pitcher, was sold to the Boston Red Sox for $20,000 and established himself as one of the finest left-handed hurlers in the major leagues. In the 1916 and 1918 World Series he set a since-broken record of 29⅔ consecutive scoreless innings. But the Babe could also hit. In 1919 the Red Sox converted Ruth into an outfielder and he led

The Miracle Worker

Babe Ruth could do it all, pitch, hit, and hit with power. After the 1926 World Series a few people even thought he could work miracles, particularly after this article (as quoted in The Complete Book of Baseball) *appeared in the October 8, 1926, edition of the* New York Times.

"ESSEX FALLS, N.J., Oct. 7—John Dale Sylvester, 11 years old, to whom physicians allotted thirty minutes of life when he was stricken with blood poisoning last week, was pronounced well on the road to recovery this afternoon after he had contentedly listened to the radio returns of the Yankees' defeat of the Cardinals. His father, Horace Sylvester Jr., Vice President of the National City Bank, and the physicians are convinced that John owes his life to messages of encouragement which the boy received Wednesday from Babe Ruth and other world series players. They had learned of his plight and of his request for autographed baseballs from his father.

The physicians say that the boy's return to health began when he learned the news of Ruth's three homers in the fourth game of the series. His fever began to abate at once, and the favorable course was hastened today after he had listened to the radio returns, clutching his autographed baseballs which he received by air mail on Wednesday night.

John's intense interest in the world series and in home runs especially were explained to his family today, when his chums told of the boy's ability on the sand lots. He had modestly refrained from mentioning the fact that he had a reputation as a home run hitter and a skillful third baseman."

---

the American League with 29 home runs and 114 runs battled in.

The Sox, however, were in serious financial difficulties, and Boston sold Ruth, their star, to the New York Yankees for $100,000 and a $300,000 loan. In New York Ruth's hitting exploded. In 1920 he hit a record 54 homers and led the league with 137 RBIs. It seemed that no one would ever have a more spectacular season, but in 1921 Ruth topped it, with 59 homers, 171 RBIs, 177 runs scored, and 144 walks. The Yankee dynasty had begun.

Prior to Ruth's arrival, the Yankees had been just another team. But in 1921 they won the first of their dozens of pennants (in the '20s they captured American League championships in 1921, 1922, 1923, 1926, 1927, and 1928). The Yankees of the 1920s were known as Murderers

Row for their power-hitting lineups. Assisting Ruth in demolishing enemy pitchers were three other Hall of Famers: first baseman Lou "the Iron Horse" Gehrig (so named because of his 2,130-consecutive game playing streak), shortstop Tony Lazzeri, and center fielder Earle Combs. In 1927 Ruth again shattered his own home run record by swatting 60 homers. All the while, Ruth caroused as much as any player ever did—eating, drinking, and womanizing while he continued to hit the longest homers ever. Everything he did, on and off the field, fascinated the public:

Boxer Jack Dempsey won forty-nine out of his sixty professional fights by knocking out his opponents.

"The harder you grip the bat," Ruth once explained, "the more you can swing through the ball, and the farther the ball will go. I swing big, with everything I got. I hit big, or I miss big. I like to live as big as I can."[46]

"The Utmost Convenient Dispatch"

In the '20s baseball faced little competition from either basketball or pro football. But boxing was wildly popular, much more popular than it is today. Jack "the Manassa Mauler" Dempsey boxed the way Babe Ruth played ball. Of his sixty professional fights, Dempsey won forty-nine by knockouts and lost just seven (with one tie). Dempsey, like Ruth, came from a tough background, and he got his start as a barroom brawler, who worked saloons and was paid in spectator contributions. In 1914 Dempsey turned pro. By July 1919 he was fighting heavyweight champion Jess Willard, whom he knocked out in the third round. Willard suffered a broken jaw, a closed eye, two broken ribs, and some loss of hearing.

In 1921 Dempsey defended his title against French boxer Georges Carpentier. Promoters ballyhooed the bout as one in which a World War I veteran (Carpentier) fought a man who had avoided military service (Dempsey). The fight attracted the first million-dollar gate in boxing history and a great deal of publicity. The *New York Times* devoted all of its first thirteen pages to covering the bout—except for a small item on page one noting the formal end of World War I. Dempsey won with a fourth-round knockout.

Dempsey was simply a boxing machine, almost mechanical in the way he bludgeoned opponents into submission. He had no fancy footwork, no showmanship—he just crashed one devastating blow after another. "He seldom moved his feet and never hopped, skipped or jumped," wrote H. L. Mencken in the *New York Sun*, "His strategy consisted in the bare business of: (a) standing up to it as quietly and solidly as possible; and (b) of jolting, pumping, thumping, bouncing and shocking his antagonist to death with the utmost convenient dispatch." [47]

Dempsey's fight against Argentinean Luis Firpo, "the Wild Bull of the Pampas," earned him another million dollars. In the very first round Firpo knocked Dempsey out of the ring and into the press section. In the second Dempsey knocked Firpo down twice before finishing him off.

The Manassa Mauler, so-named because he hailed from Manassa, Colorado, did not defend his title for another three years. In September 1926 he faced Gene Tunney (another war veteran) in Philadelphia. The middle-class Tunney was no brawler and even read Shakespeare for enjoyment, much to the puzzlement of 1920s fight fans. Tunney, however, had the last laugh, defeating the out-of-shape Dempsey in ten rounds.

Dempsey and Tunney battled again at Chicago's Soldier Field and drew boxing's first $2 million gate. There were 104,000 fans in the stadium and 60 million listening to announcer Graham McNamee's account on the radio. Even prisoners at New York's Sing Sing prison were allowed to stay up past normal lights-out to listen.

Dempsey knocked Tunney down in the seventh round but forgot to retreat to a neutral corner. That delayed the count, and Tunney rose to his feet before the referee had reached ten. It was estimated that Tunney was actually on the canvas for 15 seconds, and many believed that the famous "long count" saved him from defeat.

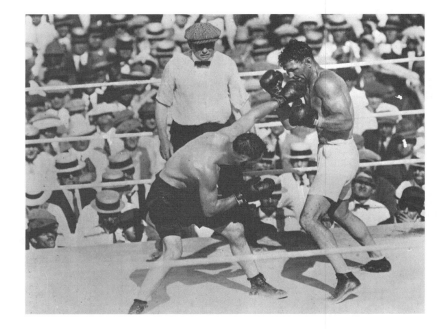

Jack Dempsey (right) fights Tom Sullivan. Dempsey eventually gave up boxing after losing to Gene Tunney in 1926.

"Shakespeare Was a Sport"

Heavyweight champion Gene Tunney was known for his intellectual nature. In April 1928 he visited Yale to lecture on playwright William Shakespeare. The Best in the World, *edited by John K. Hutchens and George Oppenheimer, contains this account of the boxer's remarks to five hundred literature students.*

"'I had heard a great deal about Shakespeare,' [Tunney] said. 'When I was in France, in a company of Marines, one of the men always talked about Shakespeare, and he would walk ten miles to get a volume of plays he had not read. I thought this tenacity must show there was something in it. So I borrowed "The Winter's Tale" from him. I read the first act, but while I knew most of the words, I couldn't get it.

'I couldn't get the meter, and it made me mad because I couldn't understand it. I realized that there were so many thoughts in so few words that my mind had not yet expanded to that extent. But here was English, written in an ordinary way, and I determined to master it. I read "The Winter's Tale" ten times, finally got the meter and knew what was going on. Today I worship at [Shakespeare's] shrine.

'It occurs to me,' he continued, 'Whether, if Shakespeare were alive today, he would be a boxing fan and would he have been rooting for me in Chicago to get up in that seventh round or stay down. Shakespeare was a sport and there is no question about the fact that he was the greatest playwright the world has ever known.'"

Tunney felt otherwise. "I can only say that at the count of two I came to," he recalled, "and felt in good shape. I had eight seconds to go. Without the long count, I would have had four seconds to go. Could I, in that space of time, have got up? I'm quite sure I could have."[48] In any case, Tunney stayed in the fight and defeated Dempsey in a ten-round decision. Dempsey—afraid of going blind from the punishing hits he would have to suffer in any more bouts—retired.

Dempsey, the "draft dodger," had not been popular with the public, but Tunney, who moved in prestigious social circles and married a Connecticut socialite, turned the fading Dempsey into a popular hero. "If Tunney's relations with the fans were poor," noted author Barrington Boardman in *From Harding to Hiroshima*, "they sank to rock bottom in 1928 when he lectured on Shakespeare at Yale."[49] The average fan believed that he was putting on airs.

The Galloping Ghost

Football in the 1920s was not nearly as popular as boxing. At the time it remained largely a college game. The National Football League (NFL) began in 1920 and often operated in such small towns as Canton, Ohio; Pottstown, Pennsylvania; and Decatur, Illinois.

Harold "Red" Grange was considered football's greatest player. He thought he would have trouble making the University of Illinois team, but in his very first game he scored three touchdowns, with runs of 12, 35, and 60 yards.

Perhaps Grange's most spectacular afternoon came on October 31, 1925. Against Pennsylvania, the 172-pound Grange, the Galloping Ghost, amazed 65,000 fans by running for 363 of University of Illinois's 400 yards as his young team walloped Pennsylvania 24-2.

"No word can paint an accurate picture of the way he jumped to top speed," marveled sportswriter George Daley, "at the way he dodged and picked his openings and slipped by tackles and changed his pace in the uncertain footing and held his feet. He was as elusive as he was fast, as daring as he was brilliant."[50]

After leaving Illinois Grange turned pro, joining the NFL's Chicago Bears. Many of his friends urged him to avoid the pro game and instead go into business or acting. But Grange's agent, C. C. "Cash and Carry" Pyle, negotiated a lucrative Bears contract that guaranteed Grange a share of gate receipts. The popular Grange helped give the often threadbare NFL instant respectability. In 1925, seventy-three thousand New York area fans turned out to see Grange and the Bears

Harold "Red" Grange was known as "the Galloping Ghost" because of his style and speed.

play the local Giants—the largest crowd to yet see a pro gridiron contest. That record was soon broken when seventy-five thousand Angelenos paid to see him perform in an exhibition against the Los Angeles Tigers. When the season—and the exhibitions—were over, Grange and Pyle had each netted $50,000. Red Grange had put pro football on the map.

Tennis, Anyone?

Another sport growing in popularity was tennis. Big Bill Tilden has been voted the greatest tennis player of all time, but in his early career he was sarcastically called "One Round" Tilden because he was so often eliminated in the first round of tournaments. In 1920, though, he became the first American to win the men's singles at Wimbledon (an honor he would capture twice more). Back home he captured six straight national singles titles (1920–1925). From 1920 through 1930 he starred on every Davis Cup team and led these elite players to victory for seven straight years from 1920 to 1926.

In 1928 Tilden committed a minor rules violation and was disqualified from the Davis Cup competition. The French were so upset that they would not see the great Tilden in action that the American ambassador to France had to intervene with the U.S. Lawn Tennis Association to secure his reinstatement.

"The Weaker Sex"

The Roaring Twenties' finest woman tennis star was Helen Wills. Because she won so often—Wills captured seven national singles titles, eight Wimbledon singles titles, and four French titles—her most remembered matches were her rare defeats. In February 1926 French challenger Suzanne Lenglen defeated her at the exclusive Carlton Club in Cannes. Great excitement filled the air. Before the match scalpers got $50 per ticket and those who were turned away made every effort to see the event anyway. "Men and women unable to get tickets . . .," wrote the New York *World*, "crept grotesquely on all fours along neighboring roofs, and police climbed trees and telegraph poles to remove the more daring of bleacherites." [51]

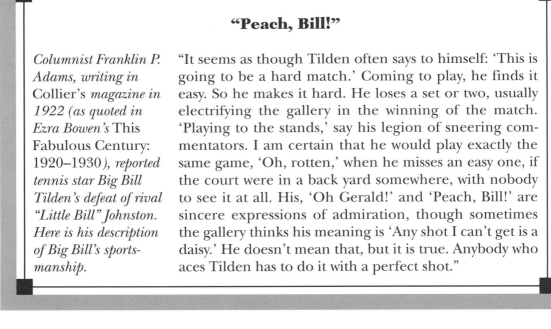

"Peach, Bill!"

Columnist Franklin P. Adams, writing in Collier's *magazine in 1922 (as quoted in Ezra Bowen's* This Fabulous Century: 1920–1930), *reported tennis star Big Bill Tilden's defeat of rival "Little Bill" Johnston. Here is his description of Big Bill's sportsmanship.*

"It seems as though Tilden often says to himself: 'This is going to be a hard match.' Coming to play, he finds it easy. So he makes it hard. He loses a set or two, usually electrifying the gallery in the winning of the match. 'Playing to the stands,' say his legion of sneering commentators. I am certain that he would play exactly the same game, 'Oh, rotten,' when he misses an easy one, if the court were in a back yard somewhere, with nobody to see it at all. His, 'Oh Gerald!' and 'Peach, Bill!' are sincere expressions of admiration, though sometimes the gallery thinks his meaning is 'Any shot I can't get is a daisy.' He doesn't mean that, but it is true. Anybody who aces Tilden has to do it with a perfect shot."

Tennis champion Helen Wills in 1929. Women made great strides in sports during the 1920s.

Helen Wills was not the only prominent female athlete. In 1926 Claire Belle Bennett became the first woman to attempt to swim the English Channel between France and England (a man first swam it in 1875). After swimming for twenty-one hours (and covering nineteen miles) exhaustion and the cold forced her to give up just two miles short of her goal.

Later that year Gertrude Ederle, the winner of three gold meals at the 1924 Paris Olympics, made her own attempt. Despite heavy storms, she began from Cap Gris-Nez near Calais, France, on August 6. Many persons believed a woman would never make it, even under the best circumstances. "Even the most uncompromising champion of the rights and capacities of women," noted the *London Daily Times,* "must admit that in contests of physical skill, speed and endurance, they must remain forever the weaker sex."[52]

Ederle started off in excellent form and by six that evening caught sight of the English coast. Then the vicious Channel tides turned, and Ederle could barely maintain her position. For three hours she struggled in the water. Then the tide turned again, and she was able to make her final push toward English soil. An hour later Ederle waded ashore, fourteen hours and thirty-one minutes after leaving France. She had even beaten the world record—set by a man—by one hour and fifty-nine minutes.

Gertrude Ederle was now one of the world's most famous athletes of either sex. She earned two thousand dollars per week

Gertrude Ederle won three gold medals at the Paris Olympics and swam the English Channel in 1924.

by swimming in special public appearances, but fame had its cost. She injured her back and was required to wear a cast for over four years. Leaky bathing caps during her constant swimming also caused her to go deaf, and she suffered a nervous breakdown. But she conquered her problems and returned to swim professionally at the 1939 World's Fair in New York. Later in life, Ederle devoted herself to teaching deaf children to swim.

The Lone Eagle

Not all heroes were sports heroes in the conventional sense of the term. The most celebrated hero was a famous aviator who pushed the boundaries of fight and excited the public's imagination.

The '20s knew no bigger hero than Charles A. Lindbergh, the Lone Eagle. Before Lindbergh, no one had flown across the Atlantic. Airplanes were still primitive, and the ocean was an immense and dangerous distance to cross. Others who had wanted to accomplish a transatlantic flight had died trying.

For years a $25,000 prize had been offered to the first person to fly across the Atlantic. In the spring of 1927 Lindbergh decided he would try to collect it. On May 10 he took off for Paris from Long Island's Curtiss Field. Others had attempted to make the flight in pairs. Lindbergh traveled alone in his tiny monoplane, the *Spirit of St. Louis.* On the way to France he battled bad weather and lack of sleep, but 33½ hours—and 3,600 miles—later he touched down at Le Bourget airfield outside Paris. An excited crowd met him in the French capital, but the reception was nothing com-

Charles A. Lindbergh poses with his plane the Spirit of St. Louis *after completing his famed transatlantic crossing.*

pared to what greeted him back in the States. Frenzied New Yorkers welcomed Lindbergh with a huge ticker-tape parade, showering the aviator with 1,800 tons of paper scraps. When World War I ended, New Yorkers had thrown only 155 tons of ticker tape. The rest of the country went just as wild for "Lucky Lindy." Businesses made huge financial offers to Lindbergh. Streets, schools, and even a town in Texas were named for him. His accomplishment, noted the New York *Evening World,* was "the greatest feat of a solitary man in the records of the human race."[53]

Most Americans would have agreed.

6 The Bill Comes Due: The Great Depression

During the twenties, faith in the economy was at an all-time high. Most investors believed that the stock market would continue to rise. In September 1929 Professor Irving Fisher of Yale predicted that stock prices were on "a permanently high plateau."[54]

But it all ended on Thursday, October 24, 1929. On that day the stock market came crashing down: 12,894,650 shares were traded—a new record—as stock prices plummeted and nervous investors attempting to dump their holdings forced stocks to plunge even further in value. Six major bankers tried to reverse the decline, but it was no use. The following Tuesday, October 29, saw 16,410,000 shares traded, a record that would stand for decades, and stock prices sank even further.

A few financially ruined Wall Street brokers and investors hurled themselves out of windows in despair. For example, when shares of the United Cigar Company fell from $113.50 a share to just $4.00 in a single day, the company's president ended his life by jumping from the ledge of a New York City hotel.

By the end of October 1929 stock prices had fallen 37.5 percent, wiping out $30 billion worth of paper profits. Those who had bought stocks on margin (paying as little as 10 percent down and borrowing the rest from brokers) were particularly hard hit.

Now they had to pay huge amounts for shares that were worthless. "How could I lose $100,000," one woman wailed to her broker, "I *never* had $100,000."[55] Trapped investors scrambled madly to sell their possessions to make margin payments. Many simply could not pay, becoming destitute.

By the middle of November the *New York Times* listing of industrial stocks had plunged from 469 to 220. By November 13 General Motors stock had tumbled from $73 a share to $36. Radio Corporation of America (RCA) fell from $505 to $28; Montgomery Ward went from $466.50 to $49.50. America's joyride was over.

Brother, Can You Spare a Dime?

Investors were not the only people ruined by the crash. When Wall Street tumbled, it took the nation's economy with it. By 1930 the gross national product (GNP) had dropped by nearly 14 percent. By 1933 it was less than one-third of what it had been before October 1929, as factories shut their doors and workers were left unemployed. The rural scene was grim as well, since farmers had smaller markets for their products.

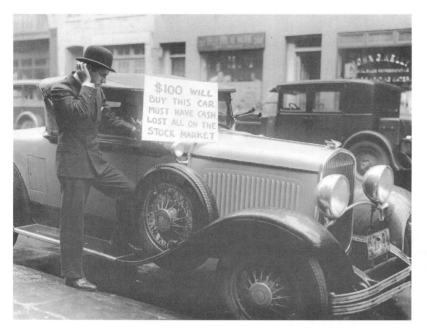

After losing his fortune in the stock market crash, a young man is forced to sell his roadster for a mere one hundred dollars.

The depression was not just measured in dollars or in economic statistics. It had a terrible human cost. Unemployment grew from 1.5 million in October 1929 to 4 million in early 1930. By 1932, the year Franklin D. Roosevelt was elected president for the first time, 13 million persons were out of work and had little hope of finding a job. A million persons left their homes and roamed the country, desperately looking for work—and their next meal. Novelist Thomas Wolfe could not help but see "the homeless men who prowled in the vicinity of restaurants, lifting the lids of garbage cans and searching inside for morsels of rotten food." Wolfe saw these men "everywhere, and noticed how their numbers increased during the hard and desperate days of 1932." [56]

Farmers were particularly hard hit. Food prices were down because so many other Americans were suddenly poor, forcing restaurants out of business and causing families to change their eating habits. By 1932 agricultural income was just one-third of what it had been just three years before. As if things were not bad enough, in the 1930s decades of poor soil conservation practices caught up with the American farmer. There had been massive soil erosion, with the result that winds blew what little topsoil was left over the countryside. Over 3 million poverty-stricken farmers picked up and moved west to get out of Oklahoma and the lower Midwest: The area, which was formerly the country's breadbasket, was now the Dust Bowl—much of it impossible to farm.

Americans were in shock. They had grown used to prosperity. As businesses closed, executives, clerks, and factory hands lost their jobs, fortunes disappeared, and homes and farms were foreclosed, people sat in stunned disbelief. The unemployed were unable to find work, beyond selling pencils and apples on street corners. Some had to beg for money or food. A popular song reflected the despair

A poor family makes its way from Dallas to Austin, Texas, in a truck that is also their home.

of the times: "Brother, Can You Spare a Dime?" Fewer and fewer people could.

Government was not much help, either. At the beginning of the depression, only local governments (cities and counties) provided money to help the unemployed. But they soon ran short as the demand for relief grew and the depression caused tax revenue to shrink. By June 1932 the city of Philadelphia completely exhausted its fund of money earmarked for relief. For three months, fifty-two thousand very poor families who had been receiving an average of $4.25 per week from the city received nothing at all. No one actually starved to death, but the poorest of the poor were reduced to horrible circumstances and lived in constant fear of the worst. As Jacob Billikopf, the executive director of Philadelphia's Federation of Jewish Charities, observed:

They kept alive from day to day, catch-as-catch can, reduced for actual subsistence to something of the status of a stray cat prowling for food, for which a kindly soul occasionally sets out a plate of table scraps or a saucer of milk. What this does to the innate dignity of the human soul is not hard to imagine.[57]

Not until September 1931 did one state, New York, begin to spend significant amounts of money to help the unemployed. In 1932 Illinois, Ohio, New Jersey, and Pennsylvania also began to assist the needy. Many state constitutions actually barred state government from directly assisting cities and counties. Many other states simply did not have the money to share with localities.

Rebuilding Businesses

During and after World War I Herbert Hoover had organized international relief programs to feed the starving people of Europe from Belgium to Russia. Elected president in 1928, he might have seemed to be the ideal person to help America overcome this catastrophic depression. But the Great Engineer seemed powerless to help his fellow citizens. He tried to rally people's hopes, but his words convinced no one. Believing firmly in business's ability to turn the economy around and put people back to work, in January 1932 he signed the Reconstruction Finance Corporation (RFC) Act, which made low-interest loans to businesses. Funded in the amount of $500 million, the RFC had authorization to raise $1.5 billion more by issuing bonds. That same month the president

The Dust Bowl

The erosion of soil in the 1930s created huge dust storms in Oklahoma and in nearby states. Avis D. Carlson, quoted in Sean Dennis Cashman's America in the Twenties and Thirties, *described one of these dreadful events in the May 1, 1935, issue of the* New Republic.

"The impact is like a shovelful of fine sand flung against the face. People caught in their own yards groping for the doorstep. Cars come to a standstill, for no light in the world can penetrate that swirling murk.

Dust masks are snatched from pockets and cupboards. But masks do not protect the mouth. Grit cracks between the teeth, the dust taste lies bitter on the tongue, grime is harsh between the lips. . . .

In time the fury subsides. If the wind has spent itself, the dust will fall silently for hours. If the wind has settled into a good steady blow, the air will be thick for days. During those days as much of living as possible will be moved to the basement, while pounds and pounds of dust sift into the house. It is something, however, to have the house stop rocking and mumbling."

A photo captures a dramatic moment in the Dust Bowl, as winds scour the dry earth and a destitute farmer.

"The Exhaustion of Almost All Sources of Aid"

In 1931, in the darkest days of the depression, many states ran out of money with which to provide relief. In July of that year, Pennsylvania reached this desperate point, and the governor, Gifford Pinchot, quoted in Albert U. Romasco's The Poverty of Abundance: Hoover, the Nation, the Depression, *wrote to President Herbert Hoover describing the situation.*

"There are more than 1,150,000 people totally unemployed in Pennsylvania today. . . . It amounts now to more than 30 percent of the normal working population. . . .

In addition another 30 per cent of our workers are now employed half time or less. Thus only about two-fifths of Pennsylvania's normal working population now holds full-time jobs.

The state is forbidden by the [state] Constitution to incur a debt of over one million dollars—and hence cannot borrow funds for relief. The levy of a graduated income tax is similarly prohibited. . . .

The Legislature last winter appropriated ten million dollars for relief. Little or nothing of that ten million dollars is left today. . . .

It is certain that the State, through the Legislature now in special session, cannot appropriate adequate funds for relief.

The State's political subdivisions are also practically helpless. Most of them have already reached the limit of their legal borrowing power. . . .

The situation in Philadelphia, with 326,000 totally unemployed and 236,000 partially employed, is desperate. Private funds are wholly exhausted. Three million dollars, borrowed by the City under special legislation beyond its normal borrowing capacity, have been spent. . . .

In the Pennsylvania coal fields during the last six months unemployment has grown 87 per cent. But in the same period the number of persons on relief increased 198 per cent, or more than twice as fast. With the exhaustion of almost all sources of aid this story is repeated throughout the State.

Growing unemployment and exhaustion of life savings and of money relief is working havoc with the health of our people. The Department of Health records a general increase of disease. . . . Twenty-eight per cent of our school children are suffering from malnutrition."

signed an act granting a government agency, the Federal Land Banks, an additional $125 million to lend farmers the money to pay their mortgages and avoid losing their land. When Congress passed a $3.2 billion relief bill in July 1932, Hoover vetoed it, but he later signed a bill allowing the RFC to lend $300 million for relief.

In 1930 Congress also increased the tariff to protect American workers from imports, but this action only hurt the economy. Foreign countries retaliated by raising their own tariffs, and American exports dropped.

All in all, Hoover's program was well-meaning and relatively aggressive for its time, but it proved to be a failure. Conditions only grew worse.

"The Only Thing We Have to Fear . . ."

In 1932 New York governor Franklin Delano Roosevelt (FDR), a Democrat, overwhelmingly defeated incumbent president Hoover in the race for the nation's highest office. Roosevelt, who came from a wealthy Hudson Valley family, was a fifth cousin of former president Theodore Roosevelt. An experienced politician, FDR had served as a state senator in New York and as assistant secretary of the navy in the Wilson administration. In 1920 he was James Cox's vice presidential running mate in the disastrous Democratic run against Harding and Coolidge. The following year polio struck Roosevelt, leaving him crippled for the rest of his life, unable to walk without the aid of crutches, canes, and heavy metal braces. But FDR bravely coped with his infirmity and returned to politics. In 1924 he

Franklin Delano Roosevelt was elected president in 1932. Americans hoped he would be able to revive the U.S. economy and end the Great Depression.

placed New York governor Al Smith's name in nomination at the Democratic National Convention. Four years later he succeeded Smith as governor.

In 1932 the Democrats nominated FDR for president. He ran on a fairly conservative platform (most of it was written by former radical-hunting attorney general A. Mitchell Palmer), pledging to cut government spending, balance the budget, and maintain the gold standard. Many thought FDR was just another genial politician, with no particular ideas to bring to the White House. "He is a pleasant man," wrote columnist Walter Lippmann, "who, without any important qualifications for the office, would like very much to be president." [58]

Nonetheless, the depression-battered public wanted a change, and Roosevelt handily defeated Hoover 22,809,638 votes to 15,758,901. In the electoral college he swamped the incumbent, 472 votes to 59. Democrats also captured huge majorities in both houses of Congress. FDR clearly had a huge mandate to do whatever was needed to fight the depression.

Once in office FDR swung quickly into action. The new president launched a wide series of reforms and relief measures he called the New Deal. He provided the nation with hope that it could finally escape the ravages of the Great Depression. "The only thing we have to fear is fear itself," Roosevelt proclaimed in his first inaugural address: "nameless, unreasoning, unjustified terror which paralyzes needed efforts to convert retreat into advance." [59]

The New Deal

As Roosevelt was being sworn in, the nation's banking system was on the verge of collapse. One of his first official actions, then, was to declare a four-day bank holiday—stopping panicky depositors from withdrawing funds and causing even more banks to run out of cash. The move worked because it gave the government time to assess which banks were solvent and reopen only those banks. Congress later passed legislation reforming the entire banking industry.

FDR followed banking reform with a slew of other new programs. The National Recovery Administration (NRA) regulated business on an unprecedented scale, draw-

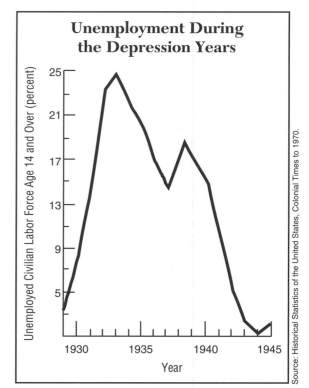

Unemployment During the Depression Years

Unemployed Civilian Labor Force Age 14 and Over (percent)

Year

Source: Historical Statistics of the United States, Colonial Times to 1970.

ing up regulations for hours and wages for individual industries from steel to poultry. The Public Works Administration (PWA) spent $3.3 billion on projects that we now describe as "infrastructure"—bridges, highways, and dams—providing badly needed work for the unemployed. The Agricultural Adjustment Administration (AAA) attempted to raise sagging farm prices and to repair the damage done by poor farming practices by restricting the amount of land farmers could till. Ironically, at a time when people were going hungry, the AAA paid farmers to plow under crops and to slaughter farm animals.

The Civilian Conservation Corps (CCC) gave reforestation and flood control jobs to young men whose families were on relief. The pay: room and board and $30 a month, $25 of which had to go home to the families. The Tennessee Valley Authority (TVA) built dams and provided electrical power to rural areas. All these programs were created during the first hundred days of Roosevelt's administration. The depression was far from over (as late as January 1937, FDR himself said he saw "one third of a nation ill-housed, ill-clad, ill-nourished"[60]), but this burst of vigorous activity raised the spirits of millions of frightened Americans.

Yet FDR's most significant accomplishment did not take place until August 1935, when he signed the Social Security Act to provide for unemployment insurance and old-age pensions for workers.

The Kingfish

Not everyone supported the New Deal. Republicans, of course, did not. Some conservative Democrats were also nervous about the new concentration of power in Washington. After all, the Democratic Party had traditionally been the party of states' rights. Many southern Democrats feared that the New Deal would challenge the laws that enforced racial segregation in their states. This did not happen, however.

Some politicians opposed Roosevelt from the left. Senator Huey P. Long of Louisiana, "the Kingfish," pushed his "Share Our Wealth" program that promised to tax the very rich and distribute the proceeds to the rest of the population. Not satisfied with the New Deal's many spending programs, Long thundered: "Not a thin dime of concentrated, bloated, pompous wealth, massed in the hands of a few people, has been raked down to relieve the masses,"[61] and his movement attracted millions of followers.

Long was ready to challenge Roosevelt in 1936 as a third-party presidential candidate. A savvy and realistic politician, the colorful Louisianian did not hope to win, but thought he might draw enough votes from FDR to throw the election to the Republicans. *Then* Long planned to run for president again and, in 1940, he expected to capture the White House. In September 1935, however, a local political opponent assassinated Long in the Louisiana state capital.

Repeal

Huey Long was one of the nation's most famous populists, a very vocal advocate of the rights of common people. But it was the aristocratic Franklin Roosevelt who supported the move to repeal Prohibition. As the depression worsened, American enthusiasm for the Eighteenth Amendment, never universal, eroded. Several economic reasons fueled the repeal movement. Noting that the legalization of breweries and distilleries would open up jobs for the unemployed, many also pointed out that if alcohol were again sold legally, money from taxes on liquor would provide badly needed revenue for the government. During his 1932 presidential campaign Roosevelt told crowds that repeal would "increase the federal revenue by several hundred million dollars a year by placing a tax on beer."[62]

Prohibition had also lost its upper-class appeal. Before World War I, the "best" people often supported Prohibition. But during the '20s, wealthy and upper-middle-class patrons flocked to speakeasies and nightclubs that served bootleg liquor. Few other people could afford to drink in any great quantity, since Prohibition had increased the cost of alcohol. One study found that between 1916 and 1928 the price of beer went up 600 percent. Gin cost 520 percent more, whisky 310 percent more. But many wealthy persons had taken to drinking and liked it. In a significant shift in trends, the upper classes now supported *repeal* of Prohibition. One observer noted that in 1910 the Washington State Women's Christian Temperance Union had attracted "the wives of prominent physicians, lawyers and men of commerce." By 1930, the organization "could list only the wives of morticians, chiropractors, tradesmen, and ministers of minor distinction."[63]

Immediately after FDR's election, the machinery of repeal began to hum in Congress. On February 21, 1933, a draft amendment (the Twenty-first) was sent to the states for ratification. Its purpose was

An employee of New York's Hittleman Brewery samples the company's first glass of beer following the end of Prohibition in 1933.

to repeal the Eighteenth Amendment. In March Roosevelt asked Congress to legalize 3.2 beer (beer contained 3.2 percent alcohol), and Congress complied just nine days later. In state after state referenda were held on repeal, and 72.9 percent of those who voted favored the scrapping of what once had been called a "noble experiment." In December 1935 Utah became the thirty-sixth state to ratify repeal. The Twenty-first Amendment went into effect, and the "noble experiment" was over.

Bootlegging disappeared, but mobsters merely concentrated on other sources of income—extortion, drugs, prostitution, gambling. Prohibition had helped create organized crime, and this new threat to public order easily survived the passing of the "dry" era.

One gangster who did not remain in business was Al Capone. In 1931 the Chicago crime lord was found guilty of income tax evasion and sentenced to eleven years in federal prison. While serving his sentence, however, he went insane from venereal disease and was released in 1939. He died in 1947.

Trouble Abroad

While the United States had been striding vigorously along the path to economic recovery in the years immediately following World War I, numerous changes had been occurring abroad. In October 1922 Benito Mussolini imposed a fascist dictatorship on Italy. In the early 1930s the Japanese military seized control of their island nation. In January 1933 National Socialists (or Nazis) under Adolf Hitler took power in Germany and began a decade of expansion. The Nazis believed in the racial superiority of the German people and the inferiority of Jews and Slavs (their hatred would eventually lead to the murder of 10 million people). Bent on erasing the humiliation of Germany's defeat in World War I, Hitler began a policy of territorial expansion and aggression by annexing German-speaking Austria in 1938. Later that year he demanded that Czechoslovakia give Germany the region called the Sudetenland, whose residents were mainly ethnic Germans. It seemed a general European war might erupt. French and British leaders flew to Munich in an effort to maintain peace. Not only did they fail to support the Czechs, they forced the Czechs to allow Hitler to occupy the Sudetenland. British prime minister Neville Chamberlain boasted that they had obtained "peace in our time."[64] Some thought this policy of appeasement was not only morally wrong but doomed to fail. "Britain and France had to choose between war and dishonor," former defense official and future prime minister Winston Churchill bitterly commented from the sidelines. "They chose dishonor. They will have war."[65]

Churchill was right. Hitler (who by now had formed alliances with fascist Italy and imperialist Japan) soon occupied the rest of Czechoslovakia and demanded the free city of Danzig on the Baltic Sea. In September 1939 (after making a deal with the Soviet Union), he invaded Poland. Britain and France declared war on Germany, and World War II began. Hitler's war machine continued to roll. In short order he conquered Denmark, Norway, the Netherlands, Belgium, Luxembourg, and France. Britain (now led by Churchill) stood alone, on the brink of defeat. Hitler was the master of most of Europe.

Adolf Hitler gives the Nazi salute to his troops in Nuremberg in 1933. It was U.S. involvement in World War II, rather than FDR's New Deal, that propelled the United States out of the Great Depression.

Meanwhile, war also raged in the Far East. Japan, like Germany, had embarked on a policy of conquest. In 1931 the Japanese seized control of the northern Chinese province of Manchuria. In 1937 Japan invaded China itself. The Chinese resisted, and a lengthy and bloody war began.

Americans did not want to become involved in another European war. It would take the bombing of Pearl Harbor on December 7, 1941, to propel them into action. Gearing up for the war effort also eliminated the depression as industry hired people on a massive scale to make weapons and ammunition, tanks, ships, aircraft, uniforms and medical supplies, and other goods required for the war effort. The twenties had been over for more than a decade. As the United States entered another war, the time of fun and spending seemed ages away.

Notes

Introduction: The Decade That Roared

1. Calvin Coolidge, *Have Faith in Massachusetts.* Boston: Houghton Mifflin, 1919, p. 202.

***Chapter 1: Boom Times:
The Economy Roars***

2. Quoted in Thomas B. Silver, *Coolidge and the Historians.* Durham, NC: Carolina Academic Press, 1982, p. 109.

3. Silver, *Coolidge and the Historians,* p. 130.

4. Paul Johnson, *Modern Times: The World from the Twenties to the Eighties.* New York: Harper Colophon, 1983, p. 222.

5. Quoted in William E. Leuchtenburg, *The Perils of Prosperity: 1914–1932.* Chicago: University of Chicago Press, 1958, p. 200.

6. Quoted in Ethan Mordden, *That Jazz!: An Idiosyncratic Social History of the American Twenties.* New York: G. P. Putnam's Sons, 1978, p. 295.

7. Joe Alex Morris, *What a Year!* New York: Harper & Brothers, 1956, p. 227.

8. Quoted in J. Joseph Hutmacher, *Massachusetts People and Politics.* Cambridge, MA: Harvard University Press, 1959, p. 127.

9. Quoted in Frederick Lewis Allen, *Only Yesterday: An Informal History of the Nineteen-Twenties.* New York: Harper & Brothers, 1931, p. 303.

***Chapter 2: Prohibition: The Wettest
Dry Nation Ever***

10. Quoted in Isabel Leighton, ed., *The Aspirin Age: 1919–1941.* New York: Simon & Schuster, 1949, p. 35.

11. Quoted in John Kobler, *Ardent Spirits: The Rise and Fall of Prohibition.* New York: G. P. Putnam's Sons, 1973. p. 207.

12. Quoted in Mordden, *That Jazz!,* p. 146.

13. Quoted in Kobler, *Ardent Spirits,* p. 224.

14. Andrew Sinclair, *Era of Excess: A Social History of the Prohibition Movement.* New York: Harper Colophon, 1964, p. 222.

15. Quoted in Sinclair, *Era of Excess,* p. 208.

16. Quoted in Mordden, *That Jazz!,* p. 146.

17. Quoted in Edward Behr, *Prohibition: Thirteen Years That Changed America.* New York: Arcade, 1996, p. 187.

18. Quoted in Jules Abels, *In the Time of Silent Cal: A Retrospective History of the 1920s.* New York: G. P. Putnam's Sons, 1969, p. 93.

19. Quoted in Sinclair, *Era of Excess,* p. 182.

20. Quoted in Fletcher Dobyns, *The Amazing Story of Repeal: An Exposé of the Power of Propaganda.* Chicago: Willett, Clark, 1940, p. 255.

21. Quoted in Leighton, *The Aspirin Age,* p. 38.

22. Abels, *In the Time of Silent Cal,* p. 81.

23. Sinclair, *Era of Excess,* p. 397.

***Chapter 3: A Controversial Decade:
From Presidential Scandals to
a Monkey Trial***

24. Quoted in Andrew Sinclair, *The Available Man: Warren Harding.* New York: Macmillan, 1965, p. 188.

25. Quoted in Johnson, *Modern Times,* p. 217.

26. Quoted in Leighton, *The Aspirin Age,* pp. 98–99.

27. Sinclair, *The Available Man,* p. 262.

28. Quoted in Allen, *Only Yesterday,* p. 201.

29. Quoted in Loren Baritz, ed., *The Culture of the Twenties.* Indianapolis: Bobbs-Merrill, 1970, p. 180.

30. Quoted in Allen, *Only Yesterday,* p. 205.

31. Quoted in Francis Russell, *Tragedy in Dedham: The Story of the Sacco-Vanzetti Case.* New York: McGraw-Hill, 1962, p. 391.

32. Quoted in William Benton, ed., *The Annals of America,* vol. 15. Chicago: Encyclopaedia Britannica, 1968, p. 530.

33. Quoted in Michael Williams, *The Shadow of the Pope.* New York: Whittlesey House, 1932, p. 313.

34. Quoted in David M. Chalmers, *Hooded Americanism: The History of the Ku Klux Klan.* Chicago: Quadrangle, 1965, p. 297.

35. Quoted in Williams, *The Shadow of the Pope,* p. 142.

36. Chalmers, *Hooded Americanism,* p. 4.

Chapter 4: The Culture of the '20s: Silents, Talkies, and All That Jazz

37. Quoted in Ezra Bowen, ed., *This Fabulous Century: 1920–1930.* Alexandria, VA: Time-Life Books, 1969, p. 101.

38. Quoted in James Robert Parrish and William T. Leonard, *The Funsters.* New Rochelle, NY: Arlington House, 1979, p. 346.

39. Quoted in Abels, *In the Time of Silent Cal,* p. 189.

40. Allen, *Only Yesterday,* p. 212.

41. George N. Fenin and William K. Everson, *The Western: From Silents to the Seventies.* New York: Penguin, 1973, p. 173.

42. Quoted in Robert E. Drennan, ed., *The Algonquin Wits.* New York: Citadel, 1968, p. 124.

43. Quoted in Brooks Atkinson, *Broadway.* New York: Macmillan, 1974, p. 253.

Chapter 5: The Golden Age of Sports

44. Quoted in Eliot Asinof, *Eight Men Out: The Black Sox and the 1919 World Series.* New York: Holt, Rinehart & Winston, 1963, p. 223.

45. Quoted in Asinof, *Eight Men Out,* p. 309.

46. Robert W. Creamer, *Babe: The Legend Comes to Life.* New York: Simon & Schuster, 1974, p. 332.

47. Quoted in James Boylan, ed., *The World and the 20s: The Best From New York's Legendary Newspaper.* New York: Dial Press, 1973, pp. 59–60.

48. Quoted in Leighton, *The Aspirin Age,* p. 167.

49. Barrington Boardman, *From Harding to Hiroshima: An Anecdotal History of the United States from 1923 to 1945 Based on Little Known Facts and the Lives of the People Who Made History—and Some Who Didn't.* New York: Dembner Books, 1988, p. 97.

50. Quoted in John K. Hutchens and George Oppenheimer, eds., *The Best in the World.* New York: Viking Press, 1973, p. 173.

51. Quoted in Hutchens and Oppenheimer, *The Best in The World,* p. 263.

52. Quoted in Boardman, *From Harding to Hiroshima,* p. 97.

53. Quoted in Allen, *Only Yesterday,* p. 218.

Chapter 6: The Bill Comes Due: The Great Depression

54. Quoted in Ralph K. Andrist, gen. ed., *The American Heritage History of the 20's and 30's.* New York: American Heritage, p. 86.

55. Quoted in Bowen, *This Fabulous Century: 1920–1930*, p. 218.

56. Quoted in William Manchester, *The Glory and the Dream: A Narrative History of America: 1932–1972*. Boston: Little, Brown, 1974, p. 42.

57. Quoted in Albert U. Romasco, *The Poverty of Abundance: Hoover, the Nation, the Depression.* New York: Oxford University Press, 1965, p. 168.

58. Sean Dennis Cashman, *America in the Twenties and Thirties: The Olympian Age of Franklin Delano Roosevelt*. New York: New York University Press, 1989, p. 134.

59. Quoted in Cashman, *America in the Twenties and Thirties*, p. 148.

60. Quoted in Manchester, *The Glory and the Dream*, p. 150.

61. Quoted in T. Harry Williams, *Huey Long*, New York: Knopf, 1969, p. 708.

62. Quoted in Behr, *Prohibition*, p. 234.

63. Quoted in Lynn Dumenil, *Modern Temper: American Culture and Society in the 1920s*. New York: Hill & Wang, 1995, p. 243.

64. Quoted in Cashman, *America in the Twenties and Thirties*, p. 556.

65. Quoted in Cashman, *America in the Twenties and Thirties*, p. 558.

Glossary

anarchism: The doctrine that denies the legitimacy of any authority.

blind pig: An establishment that illegally sells alcohol, sometimes used to describe an otherwise licensed establishment that illegally sells alcohol after the hours allowed by law.

bootlegger: One who illegally transports or sells goods; in the context of the Roaring Twenties, a bootlegger dealt with intoxicating liquors.

Bowery: A rough neighborhood of New York City.

crooner: A singer of popular songs.

crystal set: A very early form of radio.

dark horse: A political candidate who is given little chance at the beginning of a race but is subject to overtake the favorites later.

"dry": A supporter of Prohibition.

evolution: As used by British naturalist Charles Darwin, designates the theory that animals and plants have their origins in primitive life-forms and have changed, over many thousands of years, into more complex organisms.

fascism: A form of twentieth-century totalitarianism, with total loyalty given to a party and a charismatic leader, often marked by racism and/or an aggressive foreign policy.

Fundamentalism: A conservative expression of Protestant Christianity in which all parts of the Bible are accepted as literally true.

general strike: A labor strike in which all unions and workers strike; designed to change the policies of or to bring down the established government.

gross national product (GNP): The total value of goods and services produced by a nation's people in a given year.

isolationism: A policy of favoring national isolation and avoiding alliances with other nations.

monoplane: A one-engine airplane.

Prohibition: The legally imposed ban on the manufacture and sale of alcohol; generally refers to the federal ban on alcohol manufacture and sale of alcohol in force in the United States from 1921 to 1933.

protectionism: The policy of protecting domestic manufacturers and workers from foreign competition by the use of protective tariff.

Pulitzer Prize: An annual prize (for outstanding literary or journalistic achievement) established by the will of publisher Joseph Pulitzer (1847–1911).

rumrunner: A ship that transported illegal alcohol, or a person who operated such a vessel.

sedition: The encouragement of hostility to authority. Sedition differs from treason in that it does require violence or aid and comfort to the enemy.

segregation: The separation of a gender, race, or social class geographically and socially; usually used to describe the racial separation of black and white Americans.

slapstick: A form of comedy emphasizing physical horseplay.

speakeasy: Usually used to describe the nightclubs that sold illegal alcohol during Prohibition, but also used to designate any place (even pharmacies) where illegal alcoholic beverages were sold.

suffrage: The right to vote.

tariff: A tax on imports.

ticker-tape parade: New York City's trademark welcome for heroes: Ticker-tape or other shredded paper is showered down on the honoree(s) from the city's high office buildings.

trust: A monopoly.

vaudeville: A form of theatrical entertainment, usually a kind of variety show, popular in the United States in the late nineteenth and early twentieth centuries. Comedians, jugglers, animal acts, acrobats, family acts, musicians, magicians, and others performed on the vaudeville circuit.

"wet": An opponent of Prohibition.

For Further Reading

Mary Blockman, *Ticket to the Twenties: A Time Traveler's Guide.* Illustrated by Susan Dennen. Boston: Little, Brown, 1993. A short book with a scrapbook quality about it.

Fon W. Boardman Jr., *America and the Jazz Age: A History of the 1920s.* New York: Henry Z. Walck, 1968. A good short history of the '20s.

Len Canter, *Babe Ruth.* New York: Baronet Books, 1996. A good introduction to the Babe's life, although the illustrations leave a bit to be desired.

Russell Freedman, *Franklin Delano Roosevelt.* New York: Clarion, 1990. Illustrated biography of the highly popular four-term president.

Bruce Glassman, *The Crash of '29 and the New Deal.* Morristown, NJ: Silver Burnett, 1986. A brief book centering on the stock market crash and the resulting economic calamity; contains a slight amount of material on the prosperous decade that preceded it.

Joy Hakim, *War, Peace, and All That Jazz.* New York: Oxford University Press, 1995. Part of a ten-volume history of the United States. Lavishly illustrated history of the '20s, '30s, and World War II. The book is marred, however, by several factual errors.

Zachary Kent, *Calvin Coolidge.* Chicago: Childrens Press, 1988. An unusually well illustrated look at our thirtieth president. Part of the Encyclopedia of the Presidents series.

Don Nardo, *The Scopes Trial.* San Diego: Lucent Books, 1996. A retelling of the dramatic events of the trial, filled with primary source quotes.

Alfred Steinberg, *Herbert Hoover.* New York: G. P. Putnam's Sons, 1967. A straightforward biography of the humanitarian, secretary of commerce, and president.

Gail B. Stewart, *World War I.* San Diego: Lucent Books, 1991. Part of the America's Wars series.

Author's Note: The following films are available on video and are valuable sources of deeper insight into the Roaring Twenties.

The Cocoanuts (1929), with the Marx Brothers, Kay Francis, Oscar Shaw, and Margaret Dumont; directed by Joseph Santley and Robert Florey. One of the earliest talkies, this film reveals what a Broadway show of the 1920s looked like.

Eight Men Out (1988), with John Cusack, Clifton James, Michael Lerner, and Christopher Lloyd; directed by John Sayles. The story of baseball's Black Sox scandal of 1919. Quite factual.

Elmer Gantry (1960), with Burt Lancaster, Jean Simmons, Dean Jagger, and Arthur Kennedy; directed by Richard Brooks. Lancaster won an Oscar for his portrayal of a flawed 1920s evangelist.

The Golden Age of Comedy (1957), compiled by Robert Youngson. A look at some of the best silent comics of the 1920s: Laurel and Hardy, Ben Turpin, Will Rogers, and Harry Langdon.

Inherit the Wind (1960), with Spencer Tracy, Fredric March, Gene Kelly, and Florence Eldridge; directed by Stanley Kramer. The story of the famed Scopes "monkey trial."

The Jazz Singer (1927), with Al Jolson, May McAvoy, Warner Oland, and Eugenie Besserer; directed by Alan Crosland. The film that gave movies their voice.

Rhapsody in Blue (1945), with Robert Alda, Joan Leslie, Alexis Smith, and Oscar Levant; directed by Irving Rapper. Contains a nearly complete performance by pianist Levant of Gershwin's *Rhapsody in Blue*.

Scarface (1932), with Paul Muni, Ann Dvorak, George Raft, and Boris Karloff; directed by Howard Hawks. One of the earlier films to portray the gangsters of the 1920s.

The Sheik (1921), with Rudolph Valentino, Agnes Ayres, Adolphe Menjou, and Walter Long; directed by George Medford. Twenties heartthrob Rudolph Valentino's most famous film.

For excellent collections of 1920s-style jazz the following CDs are recommended:

King Oliver and His Orchestra (1929–1930), RCA Records, 1992. This two-disc set faithfully presents thirty-two songs by one of the most popular jazz bands of the time.

RCA Victor 80th Anniversary: The First Label in Jazz, Vol. 1, 1917–1929, RCA Records, 1997. Contains selections from such popular bands as King Oliver, Paul Whiteman & His Orchestra, Jelly Roll Morton's Red Hot Peppers, and Duke Ellington & His Orchestra. A very well remastered collection.

Works Consulted

Jules Abels, *In the Time of Silent Cal: A Retrospective History of the 1920's.* New York: G. P. Putnam's Sons, 1969. A lively and well-researched history of the 1920s.

Frederick Lewis Allen, *Only Yesterday: An Informal History of the Nineteen-Twenties.* New York: Harper & Brothers, 1931. The most famous history of the 1920s, but not as well done as Jules Abels's lesser-known *In the Time of Silent Cal.*

Ralph K. Andrist, gen. ed., *The American Heritage History of the 20's and 30's.* New York: American Heritage, 1970. A fine pictorial history of the two decades.

Eliot Asinof, *Eight Men Out: The Black Sox and the 1919 World Series.* New York: Holt, Rinehart & Winston, 1963. The definitive work on the fixing of the 1919 World Series—nonfiction but reads with the excitement of a novel.

Brooks Atkinson, *Broadway.* New York: Macmillan, 1974. The classic history of the Broadway stage.

Loren Baritz, ed., *The Culture of the Twenties.* Indianapolis: Bobbs-Merrill, 1970, An interesting collection of original documents from the 1920s.

Edward Behr, *Prohibition: Thirteen Years That Changed America.* New York: Arcade, 1996. Not nearly as good as John Kobler's *Ardent Spirits: The Rise and Fall of Prohibition* and Andrew Sinclair's *Era of Excess: A Social History of the Prohibition Movement.*

William Benton, ed., *The Annals of America.* Vol. 15. Chicago: Encyclopaedia Britannica, 1968. An eighteen-volume collection of many of the most important documents and writings in American history.

Barrington Boardman, *From Harding to Hiroshima: An Anecdotal History of the United States from 1923 to 1945 Based on Little Known Facts and the Lives of the People Who Made History—and Some Who Didn't.* New York: Dembner, 1988. A year-by-year look at America through most of the '20s and beyond.

Ezra Bowen, ed., *This Fabulous Century: 1920–1930.* Alexandria, VA: Time-Life Books, 1969. Part of a long series on the twentieth century. A beautifully produced coffee-table book on the '20s.

James Boylan, ed., *The World and the 20s: The Best from New York's Legendary Newspaper.* New York: Dial Press, 1973. A collection of articles from the New York *World.*

Bob Carroll et al., *Total Football: The Official Encyclopedia of the National Football League.* New York: HarperCollins, 1997. Contains sections on the development of the NFL and its history in the 1920s.

Sean Dennis Cashman, *America in the Twenties and Thirties: The Olympian Age of Franklin Delano Roosevelt.* New York: New York University Press, 1989. A textbooklike study of the '20s and '30s.

CD Sourcebook of American History. Mesa, AZ: Candlelight, 1994. An extensive collection of original historical documents on CD-ROM.

David M. Chalmers, *Hooded Americanism: The History of the Ku Klux Klan.* Chicago: Quadrangle, 1965. The standard history of the KKK; very well done.

Lester Cohen, *The New York Graphic: The World's Zaniest Newspaper*. Philadelphia: Chilton, 1964. The story of New York City's wildest tabloid.

Alistair Cooke, ed., *The Vintage Mencken*. New York: Vintage Books, 1955. A collection of writings by the most famous journalist of the '20s.

Calvin Coolidge, *The Autobiography of Calvin Coolidge*. New York: Cosmopolitan, 1929. Coolidge's own story, with an emphasis on his early life and career.

———, *Have Faith in Massachusetts*. Boston: Houghton Mifflin, 1919. A collection of speeches Coolidge gave before he became president.

Robert W. Creamer, *Babe: The Legend Comes to Life*. New York: Simon & Schuster, 1974. The definitive biography of America's greatest sports hero. Very well researched and written.

Jonathan Daniels, *The Time Between the Wars: Armistice to Pearl Harbor*. Garden City, NY: Doubleday, 1966. A very competent history of the '20s and '30s.

Fletcher Dobyns, *The Amazing Story of Repeal: An Exposé of the Power of Propaganda*. Chicago: Willett, Clark, 1940. A look at Prohibition from a dry viewpoint.

Robert E. Drennan, ed., *The Algonquin Wits*. New York: Citadel, 1968. A collection of quotes, wisecracks, and anecdotes from the celebrities who made up the Round Table at New York's Algonquin Hotel.

Lynn Dumenil, *Modern Temper: American Culture and Society in the 1920s*. New York: Hill & Wang, 1995. A look at 1920s cultural issues.

George N. Fenin and William K. Everson, *The Western: From Silents to the Seventies*. New York: Penguin, 1973. A scholarly yet highly readable history of the western film genre.

Louis Filler, ed., *The President Speaks: From McKinley to Lyndon Johnson*. New York: G. P. Putnam's Sons, 1964. A collection of notable presidential speeches.

Margaret Case Harriman, *The Vicious Circle: The Story of the Algonquin Round Table*. New York: Rinehart, 1951. A history of the Algonquin wits, told by the daughter of the owner of the hotel.

John K. Hutchens and George Oppenheimer, eds., *The Best in the World*. New York: Viking Press, 1973. Collection of articles from the New York *World*. Very similar to Boylan's *The World and the 20s*.

J. Joseph Hutmacher, *Massachusetts People and Politics*. Cambridge, MA: Harvard University Press, 1959. Explains how the immigrant vote shifted from Republican to Democrat in Massachusetts—and the nation—during the 1920s.

Paul Johnson, *Modern Times: The World from the Twenties to the Eighties*. New York: Harper Colophon, 1983. A brilliantly executed general history of the twentieth century with an interesting—and definitely different—chapter on Harding and Coolidge.

Kiplinger's Looking Ahead. Washington, DC: Kiplinger Books, 1993. Excerpts from *Kiplinger's Washington Letter*, including some commentary on the prosperity of the 1920s.

John Kobler, *Ardent Spirits: The Rise and Fall of Prohibition*. New York: G. P. Putnam's Sons, 1973. A very well written and researched history of Prohibition.

———, *Capone: The Life and World of Al Capone*. New York: G. P. Putnam's Sons,

1971. A biography of the famous Chicago gangster and a virtual history of 1920s Chicago gangsterism.

Isabel Leighton, ed., *The Aspirin Age: 1919–1941*. New York: Simon & Schuster, 1949. An anthology featuring articles on a wide range of Roaring Twenties (and 1930s) topics including the KKK, Izzy Einstein, Gene Tunney, and Sacco and Vanzetti.

William E. Leuchtenburg, *The Perils of Prosperity: 1914–1932*. Chicago: University of Chicago Press, 1958. Includes a critical look at the Republican administrations of the 1920s.

LII Collection: Historic Supreme Court Decisions (CD-ROM). Ithaca, NY: Legal Information Institute of Cornell Law School, Folio VIP Software, 1996. A wide-ranging collection of Supreme Court decisions including those in the 1930s that opposed New Deal measures.

Walter Lord, *The Good Years: From 1900 to the First World War*. New York: Harper & Brothers, 1960. A nostalgic look at the Progressive era.

William Manchester, *The Glory and the Dream: A Narrative History of America: 1932–1972*. Boston: Little, Brown, 1974. Similar in scope to Johnson's *Modern Times* but covering a shorter perod of time. Useful for covering the Great Depression and the New Deal.

Groucho Marx and Richard J. Anobile, *The Marx Brothers Scrapbook*. New York: W. W. Norton, 1973. An impressively illustrated look at the zany Marx Brothers comedy team.

Gaston B. Means, as told to May Dixon Thacker, *The Strange Death of President Harding*. New York: Guild Publishing, 1930. A self-serving and unreliable memoir by a highly corrupt functionary in the Harding administration.

Ethan Mordden, *That Jazz!: An Idiosyncratic Social History of the American Twenties*. New York: G. P. Putnam's Sons, 1978. A history of the '20s.

Joe Alex Morris, *What a Year!* New York: Harper & Brothers, 1956. Although this lively book focuses on 1929, it sheds great light on the decade as a whole.

Robert K. Murray, *The Politics of Normalcy: Governmental Theory and Practice in the Harding-Coolidge Era*. New York: W. W. Norton, 1973. A surprisingly positive appraisal of the conservative Harding administration.

———, *Red Scare: A Study in National Hysteria, 1919–1920*. New York: McGraw-Hill, 1955. The standard history of the antiradical crackdowns of 1919–1920.

Jay Robert Nash, *The World Encyclopedia of Con Artists & Confidence Games* (CD-ROM). Dallas: ZCI Publishing, 1994. A finely researched and organized study of con artists; part of a series of CD-ROMs authored by Nash.

Burl Noggle, *Into the Twenties: The United States from Armistice to Normalcy*. Urbana: University of Illinois Press, 1974. An interesting study of the last two years of the Wilson administration.

James Robert Parrish and William T. Leonard, *The Funsters*. New Rochelle, NY: Arlington House, 1979. An illustrated look at movie comedians; includes many of the silent stars of the '20s.

William Preston Jr., *Aliens and Dissenters: Federal Suppression of the Radicals, 1903–1933*. New York: Harper Colophon, 1963. Includes a look at the Palmer raids.

Albert U. Romasco, *The Poverty of Abundance: Hoover, the Nation, the Depression.* New York: Oxford University Press, 1965. An examination of Herbert Hoover's failed attempts to combat the Great Depression.

Francis Russell, *A City in Terror: 1919—The Boston Police Strike.* New York: Viking Press, 1975. This history of the 1919 Boston police strike is highly critical of the actions of then-Massachusetts governor Calvin Coolidge.

———, *The Shadow of Blooming Grove: Warren G. Harding in His Times.* New York: McGraw-Hill, 1968. An excellent and exhaustive biography of President Harding.

———, *Tragedy in Dedham: The Story of the Sacco-Vanzetti Case,* New York: McGraw-Hill, 1962. This very thorough study of the famous case concludes that Sacco was guilty but Vanzetti was innocent.

Thomas B. Silver, *Coolidge and the Historians.* Durham, NC: Carolina Academic Press, 1982. A brief but energetic defense of the Coolidge presidency.

Andrew Sinclair, *The Available Man: Warren Harding.* New York: Macmillan, 1965. Not as detailed a biography as Russell's *The Shadow of Blooming Grove,* but nonetheless a solid work.

———, *Era of Excess: A Social History of the Prohibition Movement.* New York: Harper Colophon, 1964. A fine history of Prohibition that is comparable to John Kobler's excellent *Ardent Spirits.*

Warren Sloat, *1929: America Before the Crash.* New York: Macmillan, 1929. A tediously written look at the '20s—not nearly as good as Joe Alex Morris's less pretentious *What a Year!*

Time, "Chicago's Record," February 25, 1926. An account of Chicago's St. Valentine's Day massacre.

Time Almanac of the 20th Century (CD-ROM). Cambridge, MA: Softkey International, 1995. As part of its coverage of the 1920s this CD-ROM contains an account of Chicago's St. Valentine's Day massacre.

James E. Watson, *As I Knew Them.* Indianapolis: Bobbs-Merrill, 1936. A former U.S. senator's conversational-style recollections, including the author's opinions on three presidents: Harding, Coolidge, and Hoover.

William Allen White, *A Puritan in Babylon: The Story of Calvin Coolidge.* New York: Macmillan, 1939. A critical biography.

Michael Williams, *The Shadow of the Pope.* New York: Whittlesey House, 1932. An early history of American anti-Catholicism. Features many illustrations and examples of anti-Catholic propaganda of the 1920s.

T. Harry Williams, *Huey Long.* New York: Knopf, 1969. One of the best political biographies ever written. A huge but engrossing study of the controversial Louisiana politician, enriched by many interviews Williams conducted with former Long associates.

Index

Picture Credits

Cover photo: Underwood & Underwood/Corbis-Bettmann

Archive Photos, 21, 26, 28, 29, 32, 35, 36, 54, 73

Archive Photos/American Stock, 68 (bottom)

Brown Brothers, 33

Corbis-Bettmann, 14, 18 (top), 19, 39, 49 (top), 58, 59, 68 (top)

Library of Congress, 11, 12, 13, 18 (bottom), 46, 55, 61 (bottom), 72, 75, 79

The Museum of Modern Art/Film Stills Archives, 50

Photofest, 49 (bottom), 51, 52, 53, 56, 63, 64

Smithsonian Institution, 47, 69

Stock Montage, Inc., 24, 61 (top), 78

UPI/Corbis-Bettmann, 16, 38, 41, 42, 43, 66, 71

About the Author

David Pietrusza's works for younger readers include *The End of the Cold War, The Invasion of Normandy, The Battle of Waterloo, John F. Kennedy, The Chinese Cultural Revolution,* and *Smoking,* all published by Lucent.

Pietrusza served as president of the Society for American Baseball Research (SABR) from 1993 through 1997 and is coeditor of *Total Baseball,* the official encyclopedia of Major League Baseball, as well as the books *Total Braves, Total Indians,* and *Total Mets.* Pietrusza has written five books on baseball (*Judge and Jury: The Life and Times of Judge Kenesaw Mountain Landis, Lights On!, Minor Miracles, Major Leagues,* and *Baseball's Canadian-American League*) and two works on basketball for younger readers (*The Phoenix Suns* and *The Boston Celtics*). He was managing editor of *Total Football,* the official encyclopedia of the NFL.

In 1994 Pietrusza served as a consultant for the PBS Learning Link on-line system and wrote and produced the documentary *Local Heroes* for PBS affiliate WMHT. He lives with his wife, Patricia, in Scotia, New York.